ITALIAN RAPIER COMBAT

Ridolfo Capo Ferro in the 52nd year of age

ITALIAN RAPIER COMBAT

Ridolfo Capo Ferro

Edited and Presented by Jared Kirby

TRANSLATED BY MAESTRO RAMÓN MARTINEZ, MAESTRO JEANETTE ACOSTA-MARTINEZ AND JARED KIRBY

Greenhill Books

Greenhill Books, c/o Pen & Sword Books Ltd, 47 Church Street, Barnsley, S. Yorkshire, S70 2AS, England
For more information on our books, please visit www.greenhillbooks.com,
email contact@greenhillbooks.com or write to us at the above address.

"Of all the Italian works on fencing none ever had such a share in fixing the principles of the science ... The theories which he enunciated, the system that he followed ... were hardly improved on by anyone"
– Egerton Castle, Schools and Masters of Fence

Publishing history
Italian Rapier Combat was first published in 1610. Almost four hundred years later, in 2004, a new edition with an introduction and glossary was published by Greenhill Books. It was re-released in 2012 by Frontline Books and Palgrave Macmillan. This 2021 edition, published by Greenhill Books, has a new introduction and a revised translation and glossary.

ISBN 9781784386917

CIP data records for this title are available from the British Library

Printed in China by Leo Paper Products Ltd

CONTENTS

ACKNOWLEDGEMENTS

I would like to dedicate this work to the patrons who made this possible.
Without their generous donations and patience this translation could not have come to fruition:

William Wilson, The Stoccata School of Defence, Michael Anderson, Tim Ruzicki, Craig Johnson, Antone Blair, Chris Lyon, Steaphen Fick, Dave Storrs, Fred Kutz, William S. Ernoehazy, Jr., Kevin P. Menard, Martin Reznick, Art of Combat, John Lennox, Mtre Alexander Deme, Jason Porter, The School of European Swordmanship, Andrew Feest and Duncan Fatz – Sussex Rapier School, The School of the Sword on behalf of Caroline Stewart, Jason Haggerty, Russell Figgis and Paul Chant.

I also want to extend a special thank you to Maitre Gérard Six for his generous donation of the images that are used in this book as well as for his diligent work in the field of fencing.

Lastly, for their support, time, and effort, I would like to thank the following people:

Ramón Martinez, Jeannette Acosta-Martinez, Martin Resnick, Andrea Lupo 'Sinclair', Carol Crittenden, Val Eads, Ken Mondschein, Greg Mele, Mark Rector, Richard Cohen, Donald J. LaRocca, Lionel Leventhal, Seth Cunniff, Edgar de la Vega, Jherek Swanger, Aaron and Kathleen Gormanshaw, Lenard Voelker, Michael Su, Dave Storrs, Suzanne Kirby, Patri Pugliese, The New Dawn Duellists Society, Swordplay Symposium International.

In addition, I would like the thank Carol Kirby, Evan Kirby, Russell Hogg, Cecil Longino and Antone Blair for their help and support in the second edition.

In memoriam of Dwight McLemore, teacher, mentor and friend.
Dying is a long way from dead; you will always be remembered.

NEW INTRODUCTION

In the introduction to the first edition of *Italian Rapier Combat*, I explained how every translator has to make a choice. Will they do a literal translation of the text, which may create confusion for the reader; or use clearer language to convey the author's meaning, which means a more interpretive translation? Maestro Martinez, Maestro Acosta-Martinez and I made the decision to translate the first edition "as literally as possible in order to keep the integrity and flavor of the seventeenth-century text while at the same time trying to make the material clear and comprehensible to the reader." This included the choice to keep technical terms in Italian. There is a danger that using modern terms can lead to missing nuances in the historical author's meaning. Therefore, a glossary was added to aid the reader in clarifying what Capo Ferro conveys.

Looking back on the release of *Italian Rapier Combat* in 2004, I believe we accomplished this goal very well.

Now, 17 years later (and 23 years after I started working on getting Capo Ferro translated), the world of European Swordsmanship has exploded in ways I could never have imagined in the late 90s. There are more people studying the historical treatises than ever. Clubs and schools around the world are working hard to extract the fencing systems of masters and period authors. This was the catalyst for releasing a second edition of *Italian Rapier Combat*. I believe that it is time to take the second path a translator may choose and use clearer language to convey the author's meaning.

In this new edition, we have endeavored to translate many of the technical terms which had previously been left in the original seventeenth-century Italian. In order to demarcate these as terms in their present English form, we have left them italicized. This is to make certain that the reader can still reference the author's meaning in the Glossary.

In addition to this, the book has been updated to more modern language and has been reworked to make the author's intent easier to understand. For example, in the first edition, what read as: "Having the figure marked C. *stretto* on the outside of the figure marked B., and the same figure *cavando* to strike the figure marked C. by *quarta*, the same figure noted C. strikes, with the *scanso del pie dritto* traversed on the outside of his sword, in the face next to the ear." has become: "The figure C. will *engage* B. on the outside. B. *disengages* to strike C. in *quarta*. C. strikes in the face next to the ear with the *scanso del pie dritto* traversed on the outside of his sword."

I still maintain that, when possible, it's important to "read books in the original language in order to understand all the nuances of a text. There is an expression in Italian: *Il traduttore è traditore* the translator is the traitor. Each word in a language occupies a precise place in a complex web of ideas and associations, the subtleties of which can only be fully comprehended after years of immersion in the language." That being said, most people don't have that kind of time these days. It is for all of them that we present this new second edition.

Jared Kirby, New York, 2021

Introduction

Ridolfo Capo Ferro's *Gran Simulacro dell'arte e dell'uso della Scherma* has been hailed as the pinnacle of all the Italian works on fencing. Many people consider it the most comprehensive, complete and carefully written work ever published on the Italian rapier. In his book, Capo Ferro solidifies the foundation of the principles of this art and science. These fundamental principles of fencing had been in use for hundreds of years, but Capo Ferro presented them in a clear, succinct manner which became the framework for many authors to follow.

The focus of the first half of this treatise is on the art and use of the rapier. Capo Ferro defines his terms, presents the principles in an organized manner and discourses in detail about the theory of fencing. There is a presumption in Capo Ferro's work that the reader has a certain amount of knowledge of fencing theory and a comprehension of the use of the rapier. This was written in a time when men lived and died by the sword, so the knowledge of weapons was of paramount importance. The second half of the book focuses on the practical applications of this basic theory, using 43 illustrations to demonstrate the various techniques and movements, didactically showing the martial use of the rapier, rapier and dagger, rapier and shield, and rapier and cloak.

This monumental work was reproduced many times throughout the seventeenth century. In 1629, an edition was produced which removed the backgrounds from the 1610 illustrations and added intricate artwork depicting Old Testament Bible stories. Nothing is altered from the original illustrations except the background, so instead of fighting in front of rolling hills and castles, the swordsmen are fighting in front of Noah's Ark and Adam and Eve. In this translation I have chosen to use primarily the plates from 1610 while incorporating several plates from the 1629 edition to familiarize the reader with both. I have also included five pages of the original, together with their translation.

I first became interested in translating Capo Ferro's opus eight years ago. I had heard many times that Capo Ferro was the greatest fencing master of all time. Considering the high regard in which such notable authors as Egerton Castle and Arthur Wise hold this master, I found it difficult to understand that in four hundred years no one had ever translated his treatise into English. So I began looking for a translator who would take on the project. As new books came out, such as Sydney Anglo's *The Martial Arts of Renaissance Europe* (Yale, 2000), Capo Ferro continued to be praised by modern authors. This reinforced the importance of this translation.

I met with many potential translators over the years, but after the initial meeting when they looked at the material, none of them would accept the job. There were two major reasons that translators refused to work on this project. The first reason involved the nature of the highly stylized Renaissance language. It is much like asking someone to translate Shakespearean English into modern Italian. Many of the words that Capo Ferro uses have slightly different meanings now, some words are no longer in use, and others are spelled differently in modern Italian. Therefore, the only way to find the definition is through the use of a sixteenth-century dictionary. There are abbreviations that have not been used in centuries. The sentence structure in the sixteenth century would make a modern language professor scream because the grammar has changed so drastically. It is not uncommon to find one sentence that is half a page long, as the use of punctuation was very different. For example, commas are used to break up points, where we use a period today, but a period is only used to end a complete thought, where we start a new paragraph.

The second difficulty arose from the highly technical nature of this work. Without a firm foundation and understanding of the art and science of fencing, it is very difficult to comprehend what Capo Ferro is explaining and thereby translate his true intention and meaning. After five years of searching for someone in the United States, I finally decided to employ a professional translator in Italy who was familiar with text like this. Thus the Capo Ferro Translation Project was born. I set up a fund to help raise money in order to pay this professional translator. Many scholars and practitioners of the sword generously donated to support this effort and several organizations lent their help, such as the New Dawn Duellists Society and Swordplay Symposium International.

The translator worked on this project for two years and I finally received the completed manuscript with much excitement. To my surprise and dismay, it was riddled with errors. There were words mistranslated, entire sentences missing, and very little of the material made sense. It was a glaring reminder that regardless of how well someone understands the language and is familiar with historical fencing, a full understanding of the technical nature of this type of material is requisite in order to convey the meaning of the author.

I was uncertain how to improve the quality of the translation until Maestro Ramón Martinez and Maestro Jeannette Acosta-Martinez offered to help. Maestro Martinez has spent over twenty-five years working through some of the most important Italian and Spanish fencing texts of the Renaissance. Long before he became regarded as the expert of *La Verdadera Destreza* (Spanish school of rapier), he had already been teaching Italian rapier based on his own research and the traditional system of rapier and dagger that he had learned from his master. For her part, Maestro Acosta-Martinez has spent eight years studying the Italian treatises as well. I was delighted to have such qualified individuals helping to ensure that the highest quality translation would be prepared.

The technical nature of this treatise is such that the fencing terms have been left in Italian and italicized. These technical terms are best left in their original language because their meanings cannot be conveyed by any particular English word. It is important to understand these terms in their own contexts. To help facilitate this I have included a glossary prepared by Maestri Martinez and Acosta-Martinez.

Footnotes have been kept to a minimum in this book. They are often used either to add the interpretation or opinion of the writer, which may discolor the true meaning of the text, or simply to add random facts that do not further the reader's comprehension. These can be extraneous and distracting from the intention of the text.

A translator is confronted with the dilemma of whether to translate the text literally (which may confuse the reader) or to convey the author's meaning by using clearer language and paraphrasing. This translation has been done as literally as possible in order to keep the integrity and flavor of the seventeenth century text while at the same time trying to make the material clear and comprehensible to the reader. In fine tuning the translation, we clarified the text in order to facilitate the understanding of the reader of modern English. Therefore, some necessary changes had to happen, such as updating the punctuation to modern usage, in order to help make the book easier to read.

It is always preferable to read books in the original language in order to understand all the nuances of a text. There is an expression in Italian: *Il traduttore è traditore* the translator is the traitor. Each word in a language occupies a precise place in a complex web of ideas and associations, the subtleties of which can only be fully comprehended after years of immersion in the language. However, it is simply not possible for most of us, with our busy modern lives, to go out and learn a new language on nights and weekends, especially a four-hundred-year-old form of it.

In working on this project, my comprehension of the Italian rapier has been enriched and it has provided an open window into the mindset of the seventeenth-century swordsman, whose life depended on the consummate skill acquired under the direction of one of the most famous masters in history. May all those who read this book in modern English gain the same enrichment and knowledge of Ridolfo Capo Ferro's Italian rapier.

Jared Kirby, New York, 2004

Glossary

Afalsar The act of deliberately placing one's blade in a position that will draw the adversary to take an action against it, and then deceiving the adversary's action by *disengage*.

Close Measure (*Misura stretta* in Italian) 1. The distance in *pie fermo* from where it is possible to strike the adversary only by pushing the body and legs forward without moving the feet. 2. The distance at which it is possible to strike the adversary solely by the extension of the sword arm without moving the body.

Closest Measure (*Strettissima* measure in Italian) The measure or distance from which the swordsman is able to strike the adversary in his advanced and uncovered sword or dagger arm.

Contrafinta A *feint* executed to counter the *feint*. (**Contrafinte**, plural form.)

Contratempo When one intercepts the adversary's offensive action with a counter-offensive action that is executed in a briefer *tempo* than the adversary's action.

Coprir della Spada A type of *finta* executed by covering the point of the adversary's sword with the *debole* of your sword when the adversary is found in low *quarta*. This action must be performed in a straight line.

Counter-disengage (*Contra cavare* in Italian) A response to the adversary's *disengagement* to either side of your sword. You respond with a *disengagement* to return to the same position in which you began.

Counterguard (*Contraguardia* in Italian) A *guard* assumed to counter the *guard* of the adversary. Every *guard* has a *counterguard* that is chosen for the purpose of covering the possible lines of attack from the *guard* that the adversary has assumed. *Terza* is used to *engage* the *guards* threatening the outside and *quarta* is used to *engage* the *guards* threatening the inside.

Debole The weakest or thinnest part of the blade of the rapier, tapering from the middle to the point. This is the part of the blade used for striking. See also *forte*.

Direct Line (*Linea dritta* in Italian) An imaginary line that divides the body, going through the flank together with that of the adversary's. This line is used to align yourself with your adversary.

Disengage (*Cavare* in Italian) To move the point to the opposite side of the adversary's weapon either under or over their blade. This action may be performed in the following circumstances: when the adversary attempts to strike; when the adversary attempts to, or succeeds in, parrying your attack; when the adversary attempts to, or succeeds in, executing the *engagement* or *guadagnare*; when you wish to strike;

when you wish to execute the *engagement* or *guadagnare*.

Dui tempi Two separate *tempi*. For example, two movements of the sword require *dui tempi*. See *tempo*.

Engagement (*Stringere* in Italian) 1. The act of making a firm but supple contact on the adversary's blade; done for the purpose of coming to *measure* or to uncover the adversary. This action may be used to uncover the adversary from the outside, from the inside, high or low, but always in a direct line. Usually performed in *dui tempi*. In the first *tempo* the *debole* of the adversary's sword is acquired with a *palmo* of the *debole* of yours. In the second *tempo*, the beginning of the adversary's *forte* is acquired in order to force a response. When the *engagement* is done to the inside, the sword's point looks to the adversary's right shoulder; when done to the outside it looks to the left shoulder. The *engagement* of the sword is done to seek the *measure* and the *tempo*. 2. When the adversary is found in a straight line or with the body uncovered then it is not necessary to *engage* the sword, it is sufficient to *engage* the body in the straight line without blade contact. The *engagement* of the body is done only in order to seek the *measure*.

Falso A cut with the false edge.

Falso dritto A false-edge cut beginning from the right.

Falso manco A false-edge cut beginning from the left.

Feint (*Finta* in Italian) An action with the sword that simulates an attack. It may be executed with either the edge or the point. This action may be performed to the inside or the outside of the adversary's weapon, and may be executed with your weapon in either a straight or an oblique line. It is intended to draw a specific defensive action, which you will then evade so that the actual attack may strike the side that was left uncovered by the defensive action.

Fencer (*Giocatore* in Italian) Fencer or swordsman. In terms of fencing/swordsmanship, the term *giocco* (which is the root word of 'giocatore') is used and understood as the 'interplay' of the action between the opposing swordsmen and their weapons. This term has a very specific significance. It refers to a 'player' – not in the sense of a game or sport, but in the sense of someone playing a musical instrument.

Footwork (*Passeggiare* in Italian) Fencing footwork must be done naturally, as in walking.

Forte The strongest or widest part of the rapier blade, widening from the middle to the hilt. This part of the blade is used for parrying.

Guard (*Guardia* in Italian) A posture and positioning of the arm and sword that can be used in either an offensive or defensive manner.

Guadagnare To close the line of attack, covering oneself by positioning one's own weapon along the opponent's blade, with or without blade contact.

Guardia larga A *guard* with the arm held at shoulder level, extended to the side and wide. This *guard* is mentioned in two sections: once in reference to a specific use of the dagger, and once as a sword and *rotella guard*.

Guardia di faccia A *guard* with the arm held extended with the palm of the hand facing up. This *guard* is mentioned only in reference to the use of the dagger. See description in section titled 'Some Terms of the Cut'.

Guardia di testa A *guard* used to protect the head, usually taken with the sword arm extended at shoulder level and with a slightly elevated point. This *guard* is mentioned only in reference to the sword and cape. See description for plate 36.

Guardia stretta A *guard* with the arm held extended, with the wrist somewhat in front of the right knee and the sword facing the adversary's chest. This *guard* is mentioned only in reference to the sword and rotella. See description for plate 42.

Half Step (*Mezzo passo* in Italian) A shorter step or half step.

Imbroccata A descending thrust executed from *prima* guardia to the adversary's left side with the hand position in *prima*.

Incrociate Positions of the body in which the legs are crossed.

Lunge (*Passo straordinario* in Italian) When in *lunge distance* one moves only the forward foot in order to extend the distance between the feet for the purpose of striking the adversary. See plate 5.

Lunge Distance (*Misura larga* in Italian) The distance from which the adversary can be struck by extending the sword arm and taking a step forward by only moving the lead foot. See *lunge*.

Mandritto Any cut beginning from the right side.

Mandritto fendente A descending vertical cut to the adversary's head with the true edge of the sword, beginning from the right side.

Mandritto montante An ascending vertical cut with the true edge of the sword, beginning from the lower right side and traveling towards the left shoulder of the adversary.

Mandritto ordinario A diagonal cut with the true edge of the sword, beginning from the right side and traveling from the left shoulder to the right knee of the adversary.

Mandritto ridoppio Using a *mezzo mandritto* to cast down the adversary's sword followed by executing a *mandritto ordinario*.

Mandritto stramazone A diagonal circular cut from the wrist with the true edge of the sword launched from the right side of the swordsman.

Mandritto tondo A horizontal cut with the true edge of the sword, launched from the right side.

Measure (*Misura* in Italian) The distance between two swordsmen from which it is possible to strike the adversary. It is measured from the sword's point to the adversary's body.

Mezzo mandritto A half *mandritto*.

Mezzo tempo 1.The swiftest or briefest tempo in which one can strike the adversary from *lunge distance* on the advanced and uncovered sword or dagger arm. 2. The swiftest or briefest *tempo* in which one can strike the adversary when in close measure.

Oblique line (*Linea obliqua* in Italian) Any action done off the *direct line*, regardless of which fencer executes it.

Ordinary Step (*Passo ordinario* in Italian) The normal step used while in *guard* to advance or retire, in which the body remains comfortably supported on the rear leg.

Palmo An inexact unit of measurement corresponding to the length of the hand. It is derived from the *palmus*, which was originally a Roman measurement. In later Roman antiquity, a *palmus* was 0.728 feet, approximately 8¾ inches or 22 cm. A hand's breath was an alternate method of measuring a *palmo*, which was from the tip of the extended thumb to the tip of the extended little finger. It was also the measurement of the total length of the four fingers added together.

Pass (*Passare* in Italian) To pass the rear foot in front of the lead foot.

Passata Passing of the rear foot in front of the lead foot on the attack. (**Passate**, Plural form.)

Passo The correct distance between the legs when in *guard*. (**Passi/Passe**, Plural form.)

Pie fermo To stand with your feet firmly in place.

Prima guardia The 'first' guard. Position the sword above the shoulder, with the hand held palm to the outside (your right) so that the true edge of the sword blade is upward. The cross of the hilt is vertical to the ground, the knucklebow faces upwards, and the point is towards the adversary.

Primo tempo This is the tempo in which the swordsman can strike the adversary with only one movement of the sword.

Punta riverso A thrust delivered with the hand held in *quarta*. The sword hand is held palm up, with the true edge of the sword and the knucklebow to the inside. The thrust is made to the outside of the adversary's shoulder.

Quarta guardia The 'fourth' position of the sword, which is to the inside (your left) of the thigh with the hand held palm upward with the true edge to the inside (your left). The cross of the hilt is held horizontally and the knuckle-bow to the inside (your left).

Quinta guardia A *guard* found in the section titled "Declaration of the *Guards*"; illustrated by Figure E.

Risposte (*Risposta* in Italian) The immediate counter-offensive action made in response to the initial offensive action executed by the adversary.

Riverso Any cut beginning from the left side. (**Riverse**, Plural form.)

Riverso fendente A descending vertical cut to the adversary's head with the true edge of the sword, beginning from the left side.

Riverso montante An ascending vertical cut with the true edge of the sword, beginning from the lower left side and traveling towards the right shoulder of the adversary.

Riverso ordinario A diagonal cut with the true edge of the sword beginning from the left side and traveling from the adversary's right shoulder to his left knee.

Riverso ridoppio Using a half riverso to cast down the adversary's sword followed by executing a *riverso ordinario*.

Riverso tondo A horizontal cut with the true edge of the sword; launched from the left side.

Scannatura Meeting the adversary's blade on the outside by dropping the point into *seconda* and *passing* forward with the left leg while in the same *tempo* striking to the flank by lowering the adversary's hilt with your body and hand. See plate 13.

Scanso A voidance; any evasive maneuver that moves the body off the *direct line*. (**Scansi**, Plural form.)

Scanso del pie dritto A voidance made by moving the right foot slightly off the *direct line* while turning the body. See plate 17.

Scanso della vita An evasive maneuver in which the center of the body is turned away from the attacking point of the adversary's thrusting blade and the rear leg is brought back to cross behind the lead leg. See plate 19.

Seconda guardia The 'second' position of the sword. This is even with the shoulder; the palm is held down, the true edge is to the outside (your right), the cross of the hilt is held horizontal, and the knucklebow is held facing outward (your right).

Sesta guardia A *guard* found in the section titled "Declaration of the *Guards*"; illustrated by figure F.

Settima guardia A *guard* of the sword and dagger with the dagger arm held extended forward and the sword held somewhat low and withdrawn.

Stoccata An ascending thrust executed from *terza guardia* to the adversary's right shoulder.

Stramazzone riverso A diagonal circular cut from the wrist, made with the true edge of the sword and beginning from the left side.

Tempo The measurement of intervals of time that occur within the interplay of swordsmanship. It is nothing other than the measure of stillness and motion. The quickness of the motion and the brevity of stillness do not come into consideration outside of *measure*, therefore *tempo* is only measured within *measure*. For example: it takes one *tempo* to attack by *lunge* when in *lunge distance*. Another example: as the adversary unwisely moves from one *guard* to another before he has firmed himself, his movement creates a *tempo* in which one may strike him. (**Tempi**, Plural form.)

Terza guardia The 'third' position of the sword which is to the outside (your right) of the knee with the hand held palm inward (your left), the true edge is downward, the cross of the hilt is held vertical to the ground, and the knucklebow is held facing downward.

Vita The center of the body, which is the area below the navel and above the pubic bone.

THE GRAND SIMULACRUM OF THE ART AND USE OF FENCING

BY RIDOLFO CAPO FERRO
OF CAGLI

MASTER OF THE MOST EXCELLENT GERMAN NATION

IN THE GLORIOUS CITY OF SIENA.

DEDICATED TO THE MOST SERENE LORD DON FEDERIGO FELTRIO
DELLA ROVERE, PRINCE OF THE STATE OF URBINO

IN SIENA, AT THE UNDERPORCH OF PONTANI, PRINTED BY SALVESTRO MARCHETTI, AND CAMILLO TURI
WITH LICENSE FROM THE SUPERIOR AND WITH PRIVILEGE, 1610

GRAN SIMVLACRO DELL'ARTE, E DELL'VSO DELLA SCHERMA

DI RIDOLFO CAPO FERRO DA CAGLI.

MAESTRO DELL'ECCELSA NATIONE ALEMANNA, nell'Inclita Città di Siena.

DEDICATO AL SERENISSIMO SIG. DON FEDERIGO FELTRIO DELLA ROVERE PRINCIPE DELLO STATO D'VRBINO.

In Siena, al ſopportico de Pontani. Appreſſo Salueſtro Marchetti, e Camillo Turi,
Con licentia de' Superiori, e con Priuilegi. M. D C. X.

"But the peak of achievement of the Italian tradition is reached with the work of Capo Ferro ... [He] fixes permanently the principles on which all later sword-play is based" — Arthur Wise, *The History and Art of Personal Combat*

TO THE MOST SERENE LORD DON FRANCESCO MARIA FELTRIO DELLA ROVERE SIXTH DUKE OF URBINO

Every father, (most serene Lord Duke) in order to acquire a good reputation for his children, procures for them a place in a noble Court, which provides them with the most protection possible. I do also in this present book on the Teachings of Fencing. It is from the best part of myself that I endeavour to send it to the Court, and because it is very valuable to all parts of the intellect, I beg Your Highness to grant any place for it in your court, which is a perfect compendium of the world, considered perfect, showing in itself much beauty and a great seat of majesty in the world. At the same time I dedicate it to your son, the most serene Don Federigo, entreating it to his protection. Even though he is a boy in swaddles, who plays and laughs, nevertheless he wraps us in his triumphal hands. As naked as a young Hercules with a little boy's hand, not yet equal to the purpose, he threatens Hydra and defeats the Serpent, since in his appearance nobility shines. The greatness of his forefathers, the magnanimity, valor and innumerable other virtues are seen. They have exhausted the eldest and most famous historians and rendered him above every other Prince and calling him illustrious, whose eminence truly well suffices. The accustomed virtues

AL SERENISS.MO SIG.RE DON FRANCESCO MARIA FELTRIO DELLA ROVERE

DVCA SESTO D'VRBINO.

OGNI Padre (Serenissimo Signor Duca) acciò che i figliuoli suoi acquistin reputatione, procaccia lor qualche luogo in qualche nobil Corte, e di qualche protetione, gli prouede la maggiore, che può. Così fò io, il quale trouandomi il presente libro d'Ammaestramenti di Scherma, parto della parte migliore di me stesso, procuro di mandarlo in Corte, e perche son più cari d'ogn'altro i parti dell'intelletto, suplico V.A. a concederli qualche luogo nella sua Corte, la quale essendo vn perfetto cōpendio del mondo, considerato perfetto, mostra in se quanto di bello, e di buono si trona nel mondo, istesso è dedicandolo al Serenis. DON FEDERIGO suo Figlio, il raccomando alla sua protetione, il quale, ben che fanciullo in fasce, e scherzi, e rida, par nondimeno, che ci rauuolga per le sue mani trionfi, e spoglie, e come nouello Alcide, con pargoletta mano, nō ancor pari alle voglie, minaccia l'Idra, vccide i Serpēti, poiche nell'aspetto sno generoso rilucer si vede la grandezza de suoi maggiori, la magnanimità, il valore, e l'innumerabili altre virtù, che hauno stancati i maggiori, e più famosi Istoriografi, e che lui renderanno sopr'ogni Principe, e nominato, ed illustre, alla quale eminenza li basterebbono in vero le sole vir-

of His Highness are innumerable, and in quality are so great, that he can justly be called a diligent imitator of the perfection of God. Therefore do not marvel, Your Highness, if I long to introduce my book into your Most Serene House, and entrust it to the protection of the most serene Prince, your son. However, considering the strength of a father's love, please excuse my boldness. As I certainly consider the very excellent graciousness of Your Highness and your Most Serene Blood, it is not possible but to firmly hope that, without regard for the baseness of my writings, you will fully grant your most powerful favour to them. However, if it should not be convenient for your Highness to receive them with such grace, with at least consent (of this I humbly beg with as much humility) that they are able to reside in the public room of your Royal Palace and in the other public places of your wide domain. Much glory will also be done only from being able to have a place amongst those that are humbly dedicated to serve and revere the VV. SS. AA. to whom, I pray to the Lord God Almighty, gives entire and eternal happiness.

In Siena April 8th. 1610 Di V.A.S.

Ridolfo Capoferro of Cagli,
a very humble citizen and faithful servant

tù dell'A. V. in numero, ed in qualità così grandi, che ella può venir dirittamente chiamata imitator diligente della perfettione di DIO? Non ſi marauigli dunque l'A. V. ſe io bramo d'introdur nella ſua Sereniſsima Caſa, e d'appoggiare alla protetion del Sereniſsimo PRINCIPE ſuo Figliuolo queſto mio libro; ma conſiderando qual ſia la forza dell'affetto paterno, mi ſcuſi dell'ardimento mio. Io certamente conſiderata la ſingolar benignità molto propria di V. A. e del ſuo Sereniſsimo Sangue, non poſſo non fermamente ſperare, che l'AA. VV. ſenza riguardar la baſſezza del ſuggetto, il fauoriranno compiutamente del potentiſsimo fauor loro. Ma doue pur non fuſſe conueneuole all'Altezza loro riceuere a tanta gratia, cotanta baſſezza, conſentino almeno (di che humilmente le ſuplico) che ſtar ſe ne poſſa nella publica ſala del lor Regio Palazzo, e ne gli altri publici luoghi del loro ampio Dominio, che molta gloria etiandio ſarà il poter ſolamente hauer luogo fra quegli, che ſi ſono humilmente dedicati a ſeruire, e riuerire le VV. SS. AA. alle quali prego dal Signore Iddio intera, e perpetua felicità.

Di Siena il dì 8. Aprile. 1610. Di V. A. S.

Vmiliſs. Suddito, e Deuotiſs. Seruo Ridolfo Capoferro da Cagli.

General Table of the Art of Fencing

1. First chapter about fencing in general.
2. The second chapter contains the definition of fencing and its explanation.
3. In the third, the division of fencing is embraced which deals with the first part: the knowledge of the sword.
4. In the fourth, the second part of fencing is treated, and the *measure*.
5. In the fifth, *tempo* is reasoned.
6. In the sixth, the posture of the person is treated and primarily the head.
7. In the seventh, the *vita* is treated.
8. In the eighth, the arms.
9. In the ninth, the thighs, legs, feet and the *passo*.
10. In the tenth, the defense is reasoned, and the *guard*.
11. In the eleventh, seeking of the *close measure* is treated.
12. In the twelfth, striking is treated.
13. In the thirteenth, the dagger.

TAVOLA GENERALE
DELL'ARTE DELLA SCHERMA

"In terms of combat technique, this work is one of the most influential in the history of swordsmanship" — Sydney Anglo, *The Martial Arts of Renaissance Europe*

RODVLPHVS CAPOFERRVS CALLIENSIS ÆTAT.

TO THE GRACIOUS READERS

Ridolfo Capo F. of Cagli

It is not my intention to detain you by trifling with pompous and splendid words, in recommending to you the profession of arms that I do. It is extolled in due degree to its merit, for it is praised and honored much by itself. Nevertheless it praises and commends the greatness and valor of those who carry the sword at their side with dignity. Among them today is the glorious, resplendent, most illustrious Sir Silvio Piccolomini, Grand Prior of the religion of the knights of Santo Stefano in Pisa, Artillery General, and master of the Chamber of Your Serene Highness. Therefore he is not only completely furnished with the marvellous advantage of the sword but also with every other Knightly art, as his heroic actions follow the same way, to the amazement of all, it is clearly manifested. However, returning to the sword, I say to you that it is the noblest, above all of the other weapons. In its wielding, most of the industry of the art of fencing is honorably employed. For that reason (according to my judgement) the carrying of weapons does not make the entire art alone, and is not for him who makes the essential difference of a man either completely valorous or vile and cowardly. However, it is indeed the profession that makes other people know its valorous use in legitimate defense of themselves and of their country. No one can truly do this with honor without first humbling himself and submitting to the laws and rules of the discipline of fencing, in the manner of a whetstone, refining and sharpening the valor, returning it to the height of its true perfection. For this reason this science is praiseworthy and so esteemed. It would be a rather superfluous, wasted work to take the task of recounting all of its excellence. I do not believe that I may fall to any reprehension because I have set myself to adhere to terms that are brief, infallible, and well organized precepts. I

A I BENIGNI LETTORI

RIDOLFO CAPO F. DA CAGLI.

NON è la mia intentione di tenerui a bada con pompose, & splendide parole, nel raccomandarui la professione dell'arme, ch'io fò. Essa sublimata nel debito grado al suo merito, da per se si pregia, & honora assai, & tuttauia la loda, & commenda la grandezza, & il valor di quegli, che degnamente portano la spada a lato; Tra i quali hoggi gloriosamente risplende l'Illustrissimo Signor SILVIO Piccolomini, Gran Priore della Religione de'Caualieri di Santo Stefano in Pisa, & Generale del l'Artiglierie, è Mastro di Camera di S. A. S.ma perciò che non pure è fornito a pieno, & con merauiglioso auantaggio di questa della spada, ma ancora d'ogni altr'arte Cauallerescа, come l'heroiche sue attioni appresso l'istesso, con istupore di tutti, chiaramente si manifestano. Ma per tornare alla spada, dico ella essere arme sopra ad ogn'altra nobilissima; nel cui maneggio, il più dell'industria dell'arte del la Scherma honoratamente s'impiega, perciò che secondo il mio giuditio, il portar l'arme, solo non fa l'opra intera, & non è quello, che fa essentiale differenza da vn'huomo compiutamente valoroso, à vn vile, & codardo, ma si bene la professione, ch'altrui fa di saperle adoprare valorosamente in legittima difesa di se stesso, & della Patria sua, la quale veramente nessuno può fare con suo honore, se prima non s'humilia, & sottomette alle leggi, & regole della disciplina della scherma. La quale a guisa di cote affinando, & assottigliando il valore, lo riduce al colmo della sua vera perfettione. La onde essendo questa scienza si lodeuole, & tanto pregiata, che soperchio, anzi opera perduta sarebbe voler prendere l'assunto di raccontare tutte le sue eccellenze: non credo, che in me habbia da cadere veruna riprensione

have avoided the utmost blind and obscure confusion, the deceitful and felicitous uncertainty, as well as useless and ambitious prolixity. Now, according to the knowledge of my strengths and weaknesses, I do not presume to have the felicity of success in complete response to the fervor of my ardent desire. Therefore, I made certain that my honest and cordial labor has not been made in vain, deferring myself to the paragon of those before me who deal with the same subject. In this are considered the virtue of those, from whose favour all the graces* descend to us. I firmly hope that this, my most faithful and apparent teachings, may result in being nothing less than useful and beloved to you. To me, it is a small part of that sweet wisdom of true glory which, with those grateful spirits, is always my pleasure to courteously present to anyone with a sincere heart as they continuously strive in their honorable services.

* This refers to the three graces of Greek mythology which are Agalia (Splendor), Thalia (Cheer), Euphrosina (Joy). They are three sister goddesses that are often in attendance to Eros, Aphrodites and Dionysus. They are considered the givers of charm, elegance and joy to nature, art and life.

ſione , perche mi ſia meſſo a ſtringerla nei termini di certi breui, infallibili , & ben ordinati precetti, ſchiuando al più potere la cieca & oſcura confuſione, l'inganneuole , e fallace incertezza , & la diſutile, ed ambitioſa proliſsità . Hora sì come per la conoſcenza delle deboli forze mie, non preſumo, che la felicità del ſucceſſo habbia del tutto riſpoſto al feruore del mio ardentiſsimo deſiderio, così m'aſsicuro, che la mia honeſta, & cordial fatica, non mi ſia riuſcita vana a fatto, rimettendomi in ciò al paragone di chi innãzi me trattarono il medeſimo ſuggetto. Per la qual coſa cõfidato nella virtù di quello , dal cui fauore tutte le gratie in noi diſcendono , ſpero fermamente che da queſti miei più fedeli , che appariſcenti ammaeſtramenti, ſia per tornare non meno a voi vtile è diletto , che a me vna picciola particella di quel dolce ſaggio della vera gloria, che a gli animi grati ſempremai piace di corteſemente porgere a chi con ſincerità di cuore, ſi va continuamente affaticando ne loro honorati ſeruigij.

On Fencing

CHAPTER I: OF FENCING IN GENERAL

1. There is nothing in the world that Nature, Sage Teacher and benign Mother of the universe, regards with greater foresight and more diligence than the preservation of self. As such, man, being above every other noblest creature, shows himself to have great regard to his safety. Nature provides him with singular privilege of the hand, with which he not only procures the things necessary for the sustenance of life, but also arms himself with the sword, noblest instrument of all, for protection and defending himself with it against any assault of enemy force in accordance with the correct rules of true valor and the art of fencing.

2. For this reason one can clearly discern how much the said discipline is necessary, useful and honourable to man. It may be made necessary to everyone, it is good for them, and most of all required for those armed with singular valor. They are inclined to the noble profession of the military, to which this Science is subordinate in the manner of an alternative discipline, or serving it as part of the whole. The end of the means is ultimately subjected by intention.

3. The aim of fencing is the defense of oneself, from which it takes its name. To fence means nothing other than defending oneself, for defense and protection are words with the same meaning. For this reason one should know the value and excellence of this discipline and it should be as belove as the love of one's own life and the safety of their Country, being obliged to spend it lovingly and valorously in its service.

4. Therefore, it is moreover seen that defense is the principal action of fencing. No one should proceed to offense if not through the route of legitimate defense.

5. There are four primary causes of this discipline: Reason, Nature, Art and exercise. Reason as the one that disposes nature. Nature as potent virtue. Art as a ruler and moderator of nature. Exercise as the minister of the art.

6. Reason disposes Nature and the human body towards fencing and its defense. Within Reason, judgement and will are considered. Judgement discerns and understands what should be done for your defense. The will is inclined and urged toward conservation of itself.

7. The body, which is the just servant and executor of the commandments of reason, will consider in the person of true

greatness a liveliness of the eye, and the legs. In the *vita*, and arms: suppleness, strength and quickness.

8. Nature disposes and prepares the subject. Drafting and arranging it somewhat to receive its ultimate form and perfection of the art.

9. Art rules Nature and with more security, escorts and guides it through the infallible truth and to the true science of our defense by the order of its precepts.

10. Exercise conserves, augments and stabilizes the forces of art, nature, and furthermore the Science. It produces the prudence of many details in us.

11. Art observes Nature and sees, that by the small capacity of the subject, it can not do all that is intended to do. Therefore, it considers its perfections and its imperfections in many details similar to an architect making a beautiful model. Thus it sharpens, polishes, and refines the things of Nature, reducing it little by little, until the peak of perfection.

12. From Nature, the art has grasped how to defend itself: the *ordinary step*, the *terza guardia* to stand in defense, and the *seconda* and the *quarta* for offense, the *tempo* and the *measure*, as well as the posture of a person with his *vita*, how the left leg is placed in order to defend oneself, how it is pushed forward, and carried in the right leg in order to offend.

13. Without a doubt the first offense enrages them to the fight. In the fight the *ordinary step* is seen. The *Terza*, the *seconda* and the *quarta* are also seen, which many of us do at various *tempo* and *measure* in the fight.

14. Against this offense in a fight was the art of the cudgel if no other could be found. This defense was not sufficient. I believe iron was a material fashioned from hand to hand into many diverse weapons, but one always more perfect than the other. According to the multiplying offenses, in the end, the sword was found to be the most perfect weapon, and proportionate to the correct distance, which is naturally deadly, and able to be defended.

15. The weapons, of which the length is greater than the natural distance of defense and offense, only inconvenience and are abhorrent for use in Civil conversation. Those that are very short are insidious and perilous to life. Therefore within a Republic founded in justice from good laws and from good customs it is always forbidden to carry the weapons where treachery can be born and wanton homicide is possible. Furthermore in the ancient Roman Republic, the true idea of a good government was totally forbidding the use of arms. No one, even those that were noble or great, were permitted to carry the sword or any other weapon outside of war. Proceeding against those that were found with weapons at a time of peace, as against murderers.

16. The Roman soldier, immediately when arriving at home, laid down his weapons together with the short 'habit' of the soldier and returned to wearing civilian long dress and attending to the

study and art of peace. Because no Roman exercised his body (as Sallust said) without intelligence, everyone attended beyond the study of war to one charged with peace, which was desired. The gravity of war was tolerated, but as soon as the war ended there were no more captains, no soldiers, no wages at all.

17. In these times, soldiers are a major burden for Princes, Lords and the majority of the population, much more in times of peace than of war. Because they are not accustomed to any other study than war, they hate peace, and most of the time are made authors of turbulent and wicked counsels.

18. But returning to our subject, I say that the sword is the most useful and just weapon because it is proportionate to the distance in which you naturally offend. All weapons which differ from this distance of natural offense and defense are most bestial, very adverse to nature, and therefore useless to civil conversation. One is the way of virtue and true reason, and this is laborious and harsh, from which Nature never departs to ignorance and vice. Its discourse is slippery for very many. One is the straight line which can not be done without artifice. The oblique lines are infinite, and everyone can do them. Wherefore we see in our times the multiplication of offense and defense in infinite arts. From the beginning, human industry has imitated nature, and following in its footsteps has been useful and helpful to human life. Yet as soon as it goes from the track of Nature, it commences to degenerate from the nobility of its origins, and is precipitated by the pitfall of harmful curiosity and sinks the human generation into the abyss of ignorance, bringing it from the golden age into the filth of the mire.

19. From the forces of nature, art and exercise, as efficient causes of defense whose design we have treated up till now, every advantage and disadvantage of weapons arises. It is primarily derived from the correct height of the person and length of the sword; because a man of large stature who carries a sword proportional to his body will, without a doubt, easily come to the *measure* first. In regard to this, in order to help the natural imperfection of those who are found inferior in size, I believe it is prohibited in certain countries to make a sword blade longer then others. It does not seem to be something just. He who is of superior nature will still prevail in the advantage of this art, because the privilege of nature shall suffice for him, without this one manifest indignity by wishing to make him equal with the smaller. One can not take away from him in general by assigning a sword of lesser length to him. To this end the small could by chance have other advantages of the art and exercise which forgo those of nature. In these cases human prudence is not sufficient to provide these specific things.

20. The art of fencing is very ancient, and is found in the time of Ninus, King of the Assyrians, who by use and advantage of arms, became Monarch, master of the World. From the Assyrians with the monarchy, it passed to the Persians. This exercise is praised, due to the valor of Cyrus of the Persians and arrives in Macedonia. From there to Greece, and from Greece it stopped at Rome, which (according to the testimony of Vegetius) the Field Masters of Fence was brought forth, to which the name was given, CAMPI DUCTORES, VEL DOCTORES*. It means guide or Master of the field, who taught the soldiers to strike by thrust and cut against a stake. Likewise, every day we Italians carry pride in the art of fencing, even though it is more in schools than on the field or in Military use. I attest that in these times there is more use of artillery and the arquebus during war than the sword, which does not serve like the others in the acquisition of victory.

21. This discipline is an art and not a science, if taking the word science in its strictest meaning, because it does not treat eternal and divine things which surpass the strength of human will. It is art, yet it can not be made nor wrought by hand. On the contrary it is active and ministers very strictly to the civil science; because there its effects pass in harmony with its operation in the semblance of virtue. Our predecessors did not leave anything to chance in labor or workmanship, which they used in doing the mechanical and plebeian arts. All of them, although some are renowned with the name of nobility, digress and are superfluous at great length.

* Translates as field commander or teachers.

22. The substance of fencing is its precepts of defending oneself well with the sword. Its form, order, and the truth of its rules are always and evermore true and infallible.

23. Yet it is time at last to gather all that we have said in brief words to an end. Now we come to lay the foundations of this discipline, which is its true and proper definition according to the method which we will guide and address the remainder of all of its precepts.

CHAPTER II: THE DEFINITION OF FENCING AND ITS DECLARATION

24. Fencing is the art of defending oneself well with the sword.

25. It is art because it is an assembly of precepts which are always true, well ordered, and beneficial to civil conversation.

26. The truth is arranged in the precepts of fencing. They should not be measured according to the ignorance of some, who teach and write from their long use of weapons and not through the science. Therefore most of the time they make a reasoned case from an inkling of substance, confusing the foolish with sugar and 'talking nineteen to the dozen'*. Yet it should be judged on its own and restricted to the truth of its nature.

* Defined as "to talk very rapidly or vehemently" in Webster's Encyclopaedic Unabridged Dictionary of the English Language, 1996, page. 1301.

27. The benefit to them is manifested, because teaching the method of defense that is naturally very just and honest can not be doubted as the greatest aid that brings courtesy to life, because every day its effects are clearly perceived. In as much, the sword is a weapon suited to defend oneself at a correct distance, in which one or the other can naturally offend. We see that the combatants who almost always remain in defense seldom times come to offense even as the last remedy to save their lives. If the weapon should be disproportionate, that is to say, either longer or shorter than the natural defense seeks, one should not possess it.

28. In the end, what separates fencing from all the other sciences is a good defense of oneself, but with the sword.

CHAPTER III: THE DIVISION OF FENCING THAT IS PLACED IN THE KNOWLEDGE OF THE SWORD

29. There are two parts to fencing: the knowledge of the sword and its management. The knowledge of the sword is the first part of fencing which teaches you to know the sword in order to handle it well.

30. Therefore, the sword is a weapon of pointed steel and is apt to defend oneself in the distance with peril to life which anyone can naturally offend in.

31. The material of the sword is steel, the material for defense, without another being found contrary to this. Wood is of little adequacy to repel and avoid the injuries that are done every day by one to another.

32. The form of its exterior shall be pointed, because if it were blunted, it would not serve to keep the adversary far away in a distance of natural offense.

33. Its purpose is defense, which firstly means to keep the adversary far away, so that he is not able to offend me. The function is for defense, and is especially natural, being able to be put into action without danger to those near me. In the Latin language, as already heard said by a certain learned man, defend comes to mean nothing other than to avoid, or else to withdraw from something that can harm if it comes too close.

34. Afterwards, the word to defend means to offend and to strike. It is the last and helpful remedy of defense. In the case when the enemy crosses the boundary of the first defense and brings himself close so that I have come into danger of an offence from him if I am not prepared, hence by doing this then the enemy has passed the boundary of defense, entering into that of offense. I am no longer obliged to carry any respect to the conservation of his life, coming to my turn with whatever weapon suited to my offense, yet naturally, as I say, in a distance that I can arrive.

35. The purpose of the sword is to defend oneself in the said distance. It measures his length.

36. Therefore the sword should be as long as twice the arm, or as much as my *lunge*. The length of which likewise corresponds

to this: from the sole of my feet until below the armpit of the arm.

37. There are two parts of the sword; the *forte* and the *debole*. The *forte* starts at the hilt, extending to the middle of the blade. The remainder is called the *debole*. The *forte* is for parrying and the *debole* is for striking.

38. The edges are: false and right. The right is that which is down when the hand is in its natural position. Turning it outwards or inwards, out of its natural place, is the false edge. The first place, that is to say the right edge, is known in *terza*, which is the position of the sword when in *guard*. The other, that is to say the false edge, will appear evident in the position of *terza* and *seconda*, which are placements of the sword, not in *guard*, but in striking.

39. I only divide the *debole* by the right and false edge, and not the *forte*, because this consideration does not occur on the face of the *forte*, which serves no other purpose than to parry. Yet if it should be without an edge and dull, it would not be a mistake at all, in place from the point to the *forte*. The hilt is not only to grasp the sword, but moreover to cover oneself and principally the head in striking.

CHAPTER IV: OF THE *MEASURE*

40. Until now we have spoken of the first part of fencing, which consists of the knowledge of the sword. We will begin to treat the second part presently which is its management.

41. The management of the sword is the second part of fencing. It shows the method to handle the sword and is arranged in the preparation for defense. In the same defense, the preparation and the first part of handling the sword puts the combatants in correct distance and in a convenient posture of the body to defend in time. It has two parts. The first is reasoned in the *measure* and the *tempo*.

42. The second treats the arrangement of the body's limbs.

43. The *measure* is taken by a certain distance from one point to the other. For example, in the art of fencing, it is taken by the distance that runs from my sword's point to the adversary's body, which is *lunge distance* or *close measure*. Moreover, it is taken by something apt to measure the said distance, which in the use of fencing is naturally the arm that measures all the distances. The exercise of this art has all the qualities and conditions that one is expecting to accomplish *measure*.

44. The *measure* is a correct distance from my sword's point to the adversary's body from where I can strike him. According to this, it should direct all the actions of my sword and defense.

45. The *close measure* is from the feet, or the right arm. The *measure* from the feet is from *pie fermo* or from the feet increasing.

46. The *lunge distance* is when I can strike the adversary with advancing the right foot, and this *measure* is the first closing.

47. The *close measure* in *pie fermo* is when I can strike the adversary by only pushing the body and the legs forward.
48. The *closest measure* is, when at *lunge distance,* you strike the adversary in his advanced and uncovered arm, either that of the dagger or the sword, with the left foot back, accompanied with the right in striking.
49. The first *lunge distance* is one whole *tempo* and a half, the second is one whole *tempo*, the third is one *mezzo tempo*. In respect to all three distances, according to their size they seek more or less speed of *tempo*. This is enough to have said about the *measure*. Now follows the doctrine of *tempo*.

CHAPTER V: OF TEMPO

50. In fencing the term *tempo* comes to mean three diverse things. First it signifies a proper space of motion or stillness. My need is to reach a point defined for some design of mine, without considering the length or shortness of that *tempo*, only that I reach this point in the end. As in the art of fencing, when coming to *measure* my need is a certain and correct *tempo* of motion and stillness. It does not matter whether I arrive there quickly or late provided that I arrive at the desired place. For example, I move myself to seek the *measure* and I go very slowly to find it. When my adversary is firm in his *vita* such that I find it, it is enough that I arrive somewhat late; nevertheless nothing can jeopardize my design because I arrived in *tempo*. Considering how much space I have moved myself, I note my adversary has fixed himself, thus the *tempo* equals my movement to the stillness of my adversary, and his stillness measures exactly to my movement. To this end, in his being in *guard* and in seeking the *measure*, he is only considering the correspondence of the *tempo* that the combatants, in moving and in fixing themselves, mutually consume until arriving at a certain point of *measure*. For in these said actions, the quickness of the motion and the brevity of stillness do not come into consideration, rather it is through taking the correct *measure*. It is very useful to walk, as it is said, with the shoe of lead, with the *vita* counterweighted, and resting over the left leg in the *ordinary step*. The position of the *vita* is most apt to come into consideration in regards to learning the due *measure*.
51. Following this, the word *tempo* is taken in place of quickness, in respect to the length or brevity of motion or stillness. In the art of fencing there are three distances and diverse *measure* for striking. Three separate *tempi* are also found through this. One must not solely consider coming to a certain point, but that one still arrives with a certain quickness and velocity. For the *lunge distance*, which is by advancing the foot, must be a *tempo*. That is to say a constancy of stillness or moving of the combatants' sword or body, however brief. Yet not so brief as the *close measure* of the *pie fermo* and the *closest measure* which seek an

extremely swift *tempo*. For every little bit that I move with the sword's point, and every little bit that my adversary firms himself in the distance of *closest measure*, it is enough to achieve my design, because this *tempo* is the briefest, therefore we call it *mezzo tempo*. Consequently the *tempo* consumed in striking from less *close measure* of *pie fermo* will come to be done at whole *tempo*. The last *tempo* that is employed in striking is from *lunge distance*, which is by advancing the foot, one will do a whole *tempo* and a half.

52. The first *tempo*, which is one for seeking the *lunge distance*, does not consider the quickness of motion and stillness, and therefore it is not necessary to measure it by a whole *mezzo tempo*. These manner of *tempi* are only regarded in striking, for which the position of the body in striking is entirely contrary to that which is observed in seeking the *close measure*. For the first position it is easy to go little by little to seek the *close measure*; and the other is thrown with courage and speed to strike.

53. *Tempo* is nothing other than the measure of stillness and motion. The stillness of the my sword's point measures the motion of the body of my adversary, and the motion of my adversary's body measures the stillness of the my sword's point. Now, to the end that this *tempo* is exact, it is requisite that the space of *tempo* in the adversary's *vita* firming is as much as the moving of my sword's point. For example, I find myself in *lunge distance*, with a mind to come to *close measure*. Now, having moved the my sword's point to come to the said goal, it is necessary that the adversary is firm in his body while I move myself. Thus, the stillness of the adversary's body and the movement of the my sword's point is the *measure*. Therefore, if I move myself to strike before my adversary finishes firming himself, I will move myself in vain or not without my great peril, because the *tempo* would be unequal. We pose this case: both are moving to seek the *measure*. Both are given to understand that they have found it, so both come charging in at the enemy. It will come to pass, that both will not hit because the *tempo* in which they are moving to strike is not correct in respect to the distance which one must arrive at first. In this example it is seen that the motion of my point measures the adversary's body, and the motion of my adversary's point measures the motion of my body. Therefore, in the times that it happens, many are striking one another in *contratempo*, arriving equally at one *tempo* into *close measure*.

54. The *tempo* that should be considered in *lunge distance* requires patience, and that of *close measure* quickness in striking and in departing.

55. The *tempo* of *close measure* is lost either by the lacking of nature or by a defect of the art and exercise.

56. By the lacking of nature: too much slowness of the legs, arm, and the body from which they derive; or from weakness or from too much weight of the person, as we see comes to men either too corpulent or too slender.

57. By defect of the art: when one does not learn to seek the *close measure* when it is convenient, with the *vita* loaded over the left leg, with the *ordinary step*, and with the right arm extended. These have to move in company to produce the same effect, so one must move in a correct distance. Therefore, if the the sword's point is very forward and the leg behind, or if the leg is forward and the arm is behind, then one can not carry the sword with the swiftness, correctness, and promptness that is required. For if the distance of the limbs are disproportionate when coming to seek the *close measure*, although arriving, nevertheless it can not be at *tempo* to strike, because he is lacking the best *tempo* of *close measure*, from swift correctness or promptness.

58. By the lacking of exercise: one loses the occasion for *tempo* when the person is not yet well loose of limbs; or when scholars take some wicked use by proceeding straight to the vanity of the *feints*, the *disengagements* and *counter-disengagements* and similar things of this sort.

59. From this, whose end we have spoken of now, everyone can easily comprehend this to be very false: Many say that the *tempo* is taken only from the movement that the adversary does with his body and sword. However, one needs to have regard also to my particular motion, and not solely to my motion, and that of the adversary, but also to our stillness, because the *tempo* is not solely the measure of motion, but of the motion and the stillness.

60. In concluding this material of *tempo*, I say that every motion and every stillness of mine and of my adversary together make a *tempo*, in as much, that the one measures the other.

CHAPTER VI: OF THE PERSON, AND PRIMARILY OF THE HEAD

61. The head is truly a principal thing in this exercise; therefore stationed in its due place, because it is that which knows the *measures*, and the *tempi*. Hence it is necessary that it comes to be placed where it can act as a sentinel and perceive the landscape from every side.

62. The placement of the head when being in *guard* and in seeking the *measure* is correct and proper at this time: when together with the sword it makes a direct line. For in this manner the eyes will see all the stillness and all the movements of the adversary's sword and body, and will immediately know the parts that should be offended and defended. The head stationed in said parts is therefore able to cast all its visual rays in a direct line. It is not done well if the head is held very high or very low because its rays are not shed well from every side, and thus not well prepared to take or escape the *tempo*.

63. In being in *guard* and in seeking the *measure*, the head

rests over the left shoulder, and in striking it leans over the right shoulder.

64. In being in *guard* and in seeking the *measure*, the head has to retire as much as it is possible, and in striking it is required to be pushed forward as much as it can.

65. In striking, the head will look somewhat more from one side than the other, according to when one will strike from the inside or outside, so that it comes to be covered by the hilt and the sword arm.

66. Other placements and movements of the head done in *passing*, escaping and voiding of the body, in diverse sorts of *guards* and in infinite methods of striking, cannot be admitted as good because they void outside of the *direct line*, which it comes to be called by me; the which divides my body through the flank together with that of the adversary. On the contrary, I call the *oblique line* that which runs outside of my or my adversary's body. It is from one party as much as from the other in accordance to the rule which all the interplay of fencing has to be measured.

CHAPTER VII: OF THE *VITA*

67. In being in *guard* and in seeking the *measure*, the *vita* will be bent, and balanced to the back at a slope, so that the angle which is made with the right thigh is scarcely apparent, and with the left thigh comes to make an obtuse angle, so that the left shoulder is in line with the left foot accordingly, and the right equally divides half of the *guard's passo*.

68. In striking the *vita* is pushed forward, so that the right thigh forms an obtuse angle with the *vita*, and the point of the shoulder corresponds to the point of the right foot and the thigh. The left leg is carried forward through an oblique line, extended in such a manner that the left shoulder divides half of the *passo* when it is done.

69. And when one goes to strike, the *vita* will be pushed forward in a straight line, so that by the difference of striking from the outside or the inside, depending somewhat more from one than from the other side, it is removed very little from the *direct line*.

70. The purpose for the *vita* to be bent thus is: first, because in this way you are more lengthened and more covered which is better to guard and defend the parts that can be offended because a target that is more distant is much more difficult to strike. Moreover, as well in striking it carries the attacks longer, quicker, and with more strength. Therefore, the offenses coming from far away are much more secure and best.

71. Furthermore, with the bending of the *vita*: The form that it takes in *guard*, in seeking the *measure*, and in striking is similarly considered in its *scanso*, which removes your width while the bend diminishes and your height is made narrow.

72. The skew of the body will be such that anyone does not show more than half of the chest, not only in setting oneself in

guard and in seeking the *measure*, but also in striking. For when less of the chest is shown, one travels and strikes in a *direct line* so much more, and when more is uncovered much more of the *measure* and the *tempo* are lost.

73. To those who like the *guards*, and counter*guards*, and the *engagement* of this and that, of above and below, the *feints*, and *contrafinte*, the steps by traverse, the *scansi* of the legs, and the *incrociate*, inevitably forming and moving the *vita* in many strange ways. These are as things done by chance and in no one's reasoning are they stable and truly formed, so we shall consign them to other authors.

CHAPTER VIII: OF THE ARMS

74. In being in *guard* and in seeking the *measure*, the right arm should be somewhat bent so that its superior part is extended in an oblique line and lowered so that the elbow meets with the bend of the *vita* and corresponds to the right knee. Its inferior part is somewhat drawn back and forms a straight line together with the sword.

75. In being in *guard* and in seeking the *measure*, the left arm together with the left thigh and leg make the counterweight to the *vita*, right thigh and leg. Its superior part will be extended so that it corresponds to the left knee, and meets with the bend of the left flank. Its inferior part will be somewhat gathered to assist in pushing the forward movement of the *vita* in striking, which you should not do as if it were abandoned.

76. In striking, the right arm will be extended in a direct line, turning the under part of the hand and the arm upward, sometimes inside, sometimes outside, according to the side that one is striking.

77. In striking, the left arm will be extended to make a straight line with the right arm. Turn it according to whether striking from the outside or from the inside, because every little bit that one brings the arm forward or that settles oneself in an oblique line should sufficiently diminish the *measure* and the quickness of the *tempo*.

78. The sword is regarded as a whole member with the arm. It should form a straight line with the inferior part of the arm that correctly corresponds with the bend of the right flank. It should divide the *vita* in as far as its length and width in two equal parts. Therefore, in being in *guard* and in seeking the *measure*, the reason why you have to correctly return to the bending of the flank is this: every time that you will be in this place you will be quickest to aid all of your parts that can be offended. The superior part, that is to say from the summit of the head until the bend of the flank, is proportionate to the part from under the bend of the flank until the knee (which does not happen to have regard to the legs). When in the natural distance of offense advancing the feet, you can not offend without passing too much with the *vita* into certain peril.

79. The place and positioning of the sword in striking is entirely one with that of your arm, turning the false edge upward in striking, according to whether striking from the outside or inside.

80. Take diligent heed that the the sword's point always looks to the uncovered parts of the enemy, which are the right flank and right thigh. Do not permit anyone to draw you away from this intention by uncovering the left parts which is false *measure* and *tempo* that one can take in an instant. This does not happen with the right parts that are necessarily made the target.

81. The gathered arm is not good when being in *guard*, because it does not cover the *measure* I am in well. It is likewise not good in seeking the *measure*, because the the sword's point is too far away from the adversary's body. For this reason one can not take the correct *measure*, and therefore fails to strike in *tempo*. Moreover, since the arm is withdrawn it does not keep the adversary far away at a correct distance, in as much he can strike me, and so it does not do its duty. For even as the sword is primarily out of its right place, similarly it is not useful in striking, because one can not strike in the *measure* by advancing the foot. If your point is too far from the adversary, you can not correctly take the said *measure*, which is the most excellent of the closer *measures*. It is better to strike the adversary from far away than from near. Next, it is not good for launching the attack which is discharged by pushing the *vita* forward together with the arm. It is not true that the extending of the arm increases the *measure*, but it is good with the extending of the *vita* and the step forward, because the forward leg and the *vita* in driving the arm with the sword, is rested over the left leg, over which, all the *vita* is leaned with the right leg. The left leg launches it so that the *vita* is cast forward and the thigh is over the right leg, which is exchangeable with pillars and a buttress sustaining all the weight of the *vita* thrusted forward by launching the attack.

82. The extended arm from every *guard* and in seeking the *measure* can not be shown by reason, because it forces the sword out of its correct place which is arranged to defend one's own *vita* and to offend that of the adversary. In striking it does not help the *vita* in launching the attack and it is carried with less strength. Other places and movements of the arm are not desired in the interplay to strike in a direct line.

CHAPTER IX: OF THE THIGHS, LEGS, FEET, AND THE *PASSO*

83. In being in *guard*, and in seeking the *close measure*: the right leg, thigh and foot look directly forward and inclines back in an oblique line in the manner of a slope. The left leg, thigh and foot look directly towards the left parts, with the knee as

bent as possible so that the inside part of the heel directly corresponds to the point of the right heel.

84. In striking, the knee of the right leg is bent as much as it can, so that the leg and thigh come to make a very acute angle. On the contrary, the left leg with the thigh is extended forward in an oblique line in the manner of a slope.

85. The *passo* is a correct distance of the legs, as much in firming yourself, as in moving aptly to put yourself in *guard* to seek the *measure* and to strike. In respect to the distance, the *passo* is either: entirely restricted, *half step*, appropriate or *lunge*.

86. In the use of fencing, I do not know any step that is good except the *ordinary*, in which the *vita* remains comfortable and well charged in *guard* to seek the *close measure* with a short increasing of the step. When one wants to seek with very small *passi*, the foundation is too close and weak, and it will not support the weight of the *vita*. It will be disordered unless the *measure* is sought little by little with *passi* and *half steps*. It loses the *tempo* and will not launch the attack with as much quickness. Nevertheless, these said *passi* are good as they will serve to travel outside of *measure* and to place yourself in *guard* and return to it.

87. The fencing *passo*: in our best understanding we will call it military or soldierly, and divide it into *ordinary* and *lunge*. The *ordinary* is when one is in *guard* and is seeking the *close measure*. The *lunge* is when one extends the *passo* forward to strike.

88. The *passo* with respect to its location can be considered in many ways; forward, backward, to the side, by traverse, and with the legs crossed or not. Likewise, one can move either one leg alone or both, and move the legs to do an entire *passo*, either to diminish or to shift the location in order to escape or void the *vita*.

89. In my opinion, there are only two principal ways of firming and moving oneself in respect to the legs. The first way belongs to the *guard*, to seek the *close measure* or to void. The other serves to strike.

90. *Footwork* to the side does not serve any other purpose except to make a beautiful sight, to show boldness and to survey the strength of the adversary when he places himself in *guard*. In this travelling you can be served by all the narrow *passi*. They are correct, although in my judgement, the *ordinary step* still carries the assurance.

91. Moreover, there are those who are not served by this walking to the side. When the adversary is placed in an oblique line with the sword wanting you to *engage* him from the outside, in my opinion it would be quicker to immediately seek the *close measure* in a *direct line* than to follow his interplay out of the rules. There are still some who are not served by escaping the *vita* while the adversary comes to strike you. Meet him in *quarta* and in *seconda* according to whether it happens from the outside or from the inside. It would be good to meet him if you have

considered the *tempo* and the *measure* in *quarta* and *seconda* in a *direct line* without crossing the legs.

92. The crossing of the left foot towards the right in quartering oneself is useless. It cannot be done to the left because it impedes the body and shortens the movement of the right arm in striking creating a loss of *tempo*. The *scanso* of the right leg to the left side of the adversary in order to quarter oneself is something primarily done by chance, and it is more ready to serve in a friendly assault than for a dispute or contention.

93. The *passate* are not good because they lose *measure* and *tempo*. When one moves the left leg, in that same moment the *vita*, the right leg, and the sword arm cannot move to strike with the due quickness nor without danger of a response.

94. The retreat is necessary principally in striking, because in the act of striking the *vita* is necessarily uncovered. Therefore, if I firm myself too much, it could easily come to pass that the adversary responds.

CHAPTER X: OF THE DEFENSE, OF THE *GUARD*

95. Until now we have treated the first part of the management of the sword, which has taught us the correct distance and the true position of all the body's limbs. This is required for defense. Now we will speak of this selfsame defense.

96. The defense is the second part of the management of the sword which instructs us in the use of the sword for our defense. It has two parts, the first is defensive, or the *guard*. The other is offensive.

97. The *guard* is a positioning of the arm and the sword extended in a *direct line* in the middle of the offendable parts, with the *vita* arranged well to its *ordinary step*. This will keep the adversary far away from every offense and you can offend him in case he comes near to harm you.

98. Therefore *terza* is the only *guard*. It certainly does not place the hilt outside the knee, but it equally divides the *vita* through the middle, not higher nor lower but correctly in the middle of the parts. It cannot cover but by being equally ready and near to all of its offenses and defenses.

99. The *prima* and the *seconda* are not *guards* because they are not apt to seeking the *measure* and uncover too much the *vita*, and they are not equally near to all the parts of the body that one can offend and defend. The *quarta* especially shows too much of the body, and it is a way to strike and not for guarding oneself.

100. There are three occasions which make it difficult to hit the mark; that is to say, the distance to the target, because it is hidden so that it can barely be seen through the impediment of things which obscure it, and even if he is uncovered when you are drawing near to harm him with the hit, he can cover in an instant.

101. All of these virtues are contained within our *guard*. It is

sufficient to withdraw the target and for us to remove it as such when we can by means of bending and the *scanso della vita*, then the parts can be very well covered which cannot be voided and remain uncovered. It stands ready, wanting to assist in equal distance, and thus proceeding securely to justly take the *tempo* and the *measure*, which is the ultimate perfection of the *guard*.

102. Of changing from *guard* to *guard*. It is not convenient for me to speak of it nor good to do. There is but only one *guard*.

103. The offense is a defense in which I seek the *measure* and strike my adversary.

CHAPTER XI: OF THE METHOD OF SEEKING THE *MEASURE*

104. There are two parts of the offense: seeking the *measure* and striking.

105. Seeking the *measure* for offense is when I am in the *guard* seeking the *close measure* to strike.

106. There are three methods of seeking the *measure*: while I move myself and the adversary firms himself, when I firm myself and the adversary is moving, or when I move myself and the adversary is moving.

107. The *tempo* of these actions must be correct and equal to the final bounds of the *lunge distance*, which then turns the *tempo* from seeking the *measure*. It is from this place that the *tempo* is for another action: striking.

108. If this *tempo* is correct, it is necessary that you have patience until you come to the said distance and you do not move to strike first.

109. For example: I firm myself in *guard* to seek the *measure* and the adversary has already entered the same bounds of offense. While he either circles the *measure* or pretends to strike me walking with his sword, it is necessary that I firm myself with my sword's point such that, arriving at the bounds of *lunge distance*, I will not move myself to strike first. For in this action his motion must measure my stillness and my stillness his motion. If I move from my stillness before he comes to the bounds of *lunge distance*, the *tempo* will not be correct and therefore the *measure* will not have been well sought. This motion and stillness is equal in the end, so that I arrive at the beginning of the *close measure* in one *tempo*, and it does not occur only when it is quick, but when it is equal and corresponds to the final bounds of the *lunge distance*. Thus the purpose of the *tempo* of *lunge distance* is for seeking the *close measure* and the beginning of the *tempo* to strike.

110. Many in seeking the *close measure disengage* and *counter-disengage*, make *feints* and *contrafinte*, *engagements* of one *palmo* and more of the sword, they walk from every side, they twist and stretch the *vita*, they retreat in many extravagant ways, all of which are things done outside of true reason and are devised for deceiving the foolish. These make the interplay difficult. For the *engagement* of the sword, when I cannot do otherwise in seeking the *measure* in my *guard*, it is only necessary that I *engage* the *debole* of the enemy's sword in a *direct line* with the *forte* of mine and ride it without touching, but only in striking shove the *debole* of the enemy's sword with the *forte* to the inside or outside according to the occasion of striking.

111. The *disengage* is indeed good if the adversary has me *engaged* and removed from the *direct line*. At this time it is necessary to *disengage* by retiring myself with a little ceding of the *vita* or the feet then quickly replacing myself in a *direct line* to seek the *measure* because the *disengage* is done to counter the *engagement*. As the *engagement* is done in moving the sword forward, thus the *disengagement* must be done with retiring yourself.

CHAPTER XII: OF STRIKING

112. Striking is the last offensive action of fencing, which is reached when I am at *close measure*. I move with the *vita*, legs, and arm pushed forward all in one *tempo* to strike the adversary better. This is done from *pie fermo*, or with the increasing of the *passo*, according to the size of the *close measure* and according to which is more comfortable for me to take more of the one or the other *measure*, because if by my lateness or by the fury of the adversary the first *measure* is dispersed, I am able to serve myself by the second (i.e. striking from *pie fermo*). In this case, it does not occur that the *passo* hastens more than with solely bending the right knee. It is not necessary for me to seek a closer *measure*, where one has to increase the *passo*.

113. Striking is done in three methods because I can strike my adversary while: I firm myself and he is moving to seek the *measure* or to strike me, while he firms himself and I move to seek the *measure*, or because both of us move to seek the *measure* and to strike. The only difference is that when he moves to strike me, I can strike him from *pie fermo*, because when he moves to this said effect it is hardly possible to take the correct *measure* to strike him with the increasing of the *passo*. Therefore, it is necessary that I hold to the *measure* more closely and when he moves to seek the *measure*, strike him with the increasing of the *passo*.

114. Considering the body parts with respect to the sword striking from the inside or from the outside: from the inside in *quarta* and from the outside in *seconda*, high or low according to the uncovered parts of the adversary's body when he will give me the *measure*, with respect to my sword's point.

115. While I strike, I necessarily parry together with it, in such a way that I strike in a straight line and with the body in its due disposition, because when I strike in this manner at *tempo* and at *measure*, the adversary will never strike me. Neither by point nor by cut, because the *forte* of my sword travels in a *direct line* and comes to cover all of my body.

116. The cut is of little value because I cannot strike by cut in *close measure*. I cannot do the rotation of the arm and the sword without entirely uncovering myself and without giving the adversary the *measure* and *tempo* to strike me. If anyone finds utility from the cut, they cannot demonstrate it to be better than the point when the *measure* and *tempo* are comparable.

117. On horse it is better to strike by cut than by thrust without a doubt. This is because my legs are carried by another, thus they are not arranged to seek the *measure* and the *tempo* which is necessary to push forward the *vita* and arm. Yet it is very true that I can rotate the arm at my pleasure which is the proper motion to strike by cut.

CHAPTER XIII: OF THE DAGGER

It is sufficient in this brief Chapter on the dagger to record that it safeguards oneself better. For example, if I launch the attack without being attentive to the parry and the adversary throws at me, then the dagger is best employed to avoid the *risposte*. As in everything, it brings opportunity and brings some hindrance, thus it also happens in the interplay of the dagger. One can not employ the dagger without uncovering somewhat more of the *vita* and shortening the line to strike a little. This is the end of the dagger. Without going on at such length, the art deviates from the first aim given to it then since one does different workings with the sword and dagger, which are better with the sword alone to best begin using it.

NOW WILL FOLLOW

The Grand Simulacrum on the Use of Fencing

FIRST THE DIFFERENCE BETWEEN THE ART AND USE IS DECLARED

The difference is very great between the Art and the use. It is no less than between reason and accident, confusion and good order, or science and opinion. To the purpose that one more manifestly comprehends this, it is necessary that we briefly consider and declare the definitions of the art, which I have recorded already and harkened to treat with some intelligence. It is nothing more than a multitude of useful precepts well ordered to civil conversation, because one flower is not springtime, neither is one sole precept enough to make the art. Moreover, that with whatever number of precepts in the art, they are still finally confirmed when they are useful and not useless, and are not those that are submerged in the abyss of dark gloomy falseness and deceitful opinions. For art is not governed according to its own judgement, but directs all of its precepts according to the rules which will give them the laws of truth. The truth commands the art which is not founded in air, which does not teach unless these things are infallible, and is of perpetual truth. Precepts that are not standing as paragons of these laws are not recognized by them. The use of the art is wider and considers not only the things that are true, but also takes heed of the false and many other particulars that variably happen, and by demonstrating their effects it excels for assisting many disciplines. For as much, we watch it happen every day in civil conversation, that a man is not sufficient to put into action the office or the art that he does unless help comes from those in which kindness dwells. Thus all the arts, all the sciences, and all the professions are conjoined and united between them, so that if one has need of the mutual assistance from the other, one will put into execution their teachings. Nevertheless, as in the civil use every man has his particular office apart from his house and these are well separated, thus the art and the science have their own distinct boundaries and proper precepts which it is not permissible to transgress. This same difference is between the art and the use. Anyone that teaches without coming to observe this will fall into many of the gravest errors. For example, it happens that in teaching, as much with the pen as with the sword in hand, they are long winded and very confusing and similarly contradict themselves most of the time. It is because they do not first cast a stable foundation from these infallible and well ordered precepts of the art. With much more easiness and the briefest time they could well conduct their scholars to that grade of perfection which one can desire in this science. In order to facilitate the art of fencing I have endeavoured to explain all the difficulties and extract them from the obscure darkness of confusion, compress them into the smallest instructions separated from its use in order to present and place before your eyes a few figures which declare the major part our art. I leave to others the care of investing their studies in uncertainty and the infinity of particular things which, without firming themselves in a similar fashion, we see happen daily in the use of arms. If this instability and variety of things must indeed be taught it is much better, in my opinion, in the school of hand to hand so that one remembers it is not learned with the science. However, it is time at last that we come to the declaration of some remembrances and advices along with some fencing terms pertaining to the use and our figures.

Some Remembrances or True Advices of Fencing

1. First, if you are found at blows with your adversary, you must always have the eye on the sword hand more than in other places. Looking anywhere else is false, because when looking at the hand you will see the stillness and all the movements that it does, and from this (according to your judgement) you will be able to determine what you will have to do.

OF PARRYING AND STRIKING, AND VOIDING OF THE *VITA*

2. The good *fencer*, in his interplay, must never parry without responding with a strike, nor proceed to strike if he is not assured of parrying the *risposte*, nor void the *vita* if not striking. If it comes to pass that one parry's with the dagger, when the dagger departs to parry, the sword must depart to strike.

THE VIRTUE OF THE SWORD ALONE

3. One must know that the sword alone is the queen and foundation of all the other arms. It is so much more helpful than the others, because one more securely learns to parry, strike, and void the *vita*, *disengage* the sword, *counter-disengage*, and *guadagnare* the adversary's sword in all the *guards*. In the aforesaid effects, I advise you to keep the arm well extended because you will be able to deflect all of the adversary's blows far from your body.

METHODS THAT ONE MUST HOLD AGAINST A BRUTAL MAN

4. If you have to encounter a brutal man who, without *measure* and *tempo*, hurls many blows at you with great impetus, you will be able to do two things. First, adopt the interplay of *mezzo tempo*, as I will teach you in its place. You will strike him while he hurls his point, either by cutting the hand or sword arm. Otherwise, you can leave him to proceed at emptiness with somewhat voiding the *vita* backwards, and then you instantly drive a point into the face or chest.

METHOD TO BECOME A PERFECT *FENCER*

5. For one who wishes to become a perfect *fencer* it is not sufficent to only take lessons from the Master, but it is necessary that you seek to fence with diverse *fencers* daily. If possible, you

must always exercise with those who know more than you, because through the interplay with such practised enginers you will become most perfect in this virtue.

OF THE MOST SECURE *GUARD*

6. You know that in my book of the art, I do not know any other to be good than one sole *guard* which is the low *guard* called *terza*. It has the sword level in a straight line dividing the right flank through the middle with the point always aimed for the middle of the adversary's body which has the nearest parts. It is more secure than the other high *guards*, because in the said high *guards* you can easily be struck by thrust or cut to the leg. In the lower *guard* there is none of this danger and the virtue of it is only to hurl the point to strike naturally.

OF THE VANITY OF THE *FEINTS*

7. The *feints* are not good because they lose *tempo* and *measure*. Additionally, the *feint* is done either in *measure* or out of *measure*. If it is done out of *measure*, I will not move myself, but if it is done in *measure*, I will strike while he feigns.

FROM WHOM ONE MUST LEARN

8. You have to know that there are some who quickly place themselves to teach others even though they have learned and practiced little of it. They teach without foundation, rules that are true, nor understand that the knowledge is very different from teaching and that this way of teaching is acquired with length of time. It takes a long time to know the *measure* and *tempo*. One who does not know the *measure* nor *tempo* and does not have methods of teaching can be called an imperfect *fencer*, and one must be warned of learning from them.

OF *GUADAGNARE* OF THE SWORD

9. It is not of small profit nor of little beauty to know how to *guadagnare* the adversary's sword in all the *guards*. It is also not of little importance, in case the adversary has *guadagnare* yours, to know how to recover it.

In the case that he should *guadagnare* you, you will be able to do three things. First you should never *disengage* for a final strike, nor *disengage* to parry and then strike. The other is retiring backwards with ceding the *vita* somewhat, and lowering the sword, wanting the adversary to follow you in the same *tempo*. When he comes forward to accost you and *guadagnare* again, while he moves the right foot you will be able to strike from below or above his sword, whichever will come more comfortably to you. Moreover, one must be advised that we intend to *engage* the sword as much as to *guadagnare* it.

OF STRIKING IN *CONTRATEMPO*

10. It is possible to strike in *contratempo* in many ways, but I only approve of two of them. Finding yourself with your sword in *quarta*, so that the point of it looks towards your right side and your adversary comes to *guadagnare* it, in the same *tempo* that he moves the right foot to set his sword with yours, you will push a thrust with this said *quarta*, *pass* with your left or right foot forward. The other is finding yourself in *terza*, when he comes to *guadagnare* from the outside, you will thrust from *seconda* with the *pass* as above.

OF THE *FOOTWORK*

11. The opinions of masters are many and varied regarding *footwork* with the weapon in hand. I say (according to my judgement), that the *footwork* is to the right side as to the left of the adversary. First, be advised to always move the left foot accompanied by the right. Do *footwork* in a straight line so that one foot drives the other forward as much as backwards. However, true *footwork* will always be done walking naturally, so that the point of the right shoulder is forward and carrying the left foot to the traverse, so that the point of it looks towards your left side.

METHOD OF STRIKING TO THE HAND

12. You must know that every time your adversary has the point of his sword outside of your presence, either high or low or when it faces outside of your left or right parts, you will put the point of your sword in a straight line to meet the hand, together with somewhat bending the *vita* backwards. You will advance to *measure* and when you arrive, you will push a thrust in *mezzo tempo* at the said hand by solely pushing your *vita* forward and bending the right knee thus striking him. However, you are warned that in such striking you must carry the left foot backwards accompanied with the right. Moreover if the enemy's dagger arm is advanced forward and you want to strike the hand, hold to the same order as above.

METHOD OF WITHDRAWING YOURSELF WHEN YOU HAVE STRUCK

13. Having struck your adversary by *lunge* with the right foot forward, it is in single sword as in sword and dagger or sword and cape, you will withdraw yourself by *ordinary step* according to the space behind you. If you have little space, you will only carry the right leg backwards, following the enemy's sword with your sword, but if you have space, you will withdraw backwards with two *ordinary steps* which will ultimately bring you into *guard*. This is the true withdrawing, it is good in the school usage or otherwise.

DECLARATIONS OF SOME FENCING TERMS THAT APPERTAIN TO THE USE

It is necessary for scholars to know these terms which Masters of fence use in teaching, thus we declare them in the following briefest words.

OF THE SWORD

1. In the sword, the *forte*, *debole*, false edge, and true edge are considered. It pleases some to make three equal parts of the sword, that is to say the *debole* and the *forte* which are the extreme parts, and the middle because the one is apt to parry and the other to strike. Some will make four parts of the same, yet without any evident utility. The said terms are easy and intelligibility.

OF THE *GUARDS*

2. We call the *guard* a certain positioning of the hilt of the sword. Every time it is placed over the shoulder it forms the *prima*. When it descends evenly to the shoulder it makes the *seconda*.

When it is lowered more, outside of the knee on your right side it comes to form the *terza*. When the hilt is placed inside of the thigh the *quarta* is made. These four *guards* are called principal and until here all are in accord. As far as the *passo*, the arm, the *vita,* the legs, and the line of the sword, they are of diverse opinions. Some praise the narrow stance and some the wide stance, certain ones the moderate, some extend the arm, some restrain it more or less, certain ones bend the *vita*, some straighten it, others form the *guard* putting the right leg forward, sometimes the left, some hold the sword in a straight line, some high and some low, and sometimes from one, sometime from the other side, sometimes forward, sometimes backwards, in as many lines as there are found in the world, others according to diverse occasions indifferently use all of the aforementioned manners of *guards*, just calling them *alte*, and *basse*, *strette*, and *larghe*, and other names acquired according to the capriciousness of masters.

Counterguards are namely the *terza* and the *quarta*: one is for *engaging* from the outside, and one is for *engaging* from the inside. That said, for all the *guards* there will be *counterguards* that are chosen according to the diversity of the lines of the sword.

OF *TEMPO*

3. Four sorts of *tempi* are named in the school: the *primo*, *dui tempi*, the *mezzo*, and the *contratempo*. The *primo tempo* requires that whenever I find myself in either *lunge distance* or *close measure*, I can strike the adversary solely moving the sword. For this reason it is likewise known that to strike in *dui tempi* requires at least two movements of the sword. *Mezzo tempo* is when, at *lunge distance*, I strike the adversary in the advanced and uncovered arm, either that of the dagger or sword, by point or cut, or when I strike the adversary at *close measure* as he moves to strike me or to do some other action. The redoubling of the attack is done more in *mezzo tempo*. *Contratempo* is when in the same *tempo* that the adversary wants to strike me I counter in a very short *tempo* and *measure*. It should be known that all the movements and all the rests of the adversary are not *tempi* unless at *measure*.

OF THE *MEASURE*

4. The *measure* is *lunge distance* or *close measure*. *Lunge distance* is when one can strike the adversary only with the *lunge*. The *close measure* requires that I can strike the adversary in an appropriate *passo* at *pie fermo*.

IN HOW MANY TEMPI IT IS KNOWN TO STRIKE

5. The first is when the enemy is firm in *guard*. When he raises or moves his forward foot or advances, that is a *tempo*. The next is when you have parried the blow, then there is a *tempo*. The third is as he moves himself without judgement from one *guard* to go into another, before he has firmed himself there is a *tempo* to offend him. Moreover, there is a *tempo* when he raises the sword. While he raises the hand there is a *tempo* to strike him. The last is when the blow has been spent outside of the person, that is a *tempo* for following with the *risposte*.

OF THE *PASSO* AND *FOOTWORK*

6. The *passo* is called: *ordinary*, *lunge*, appropriate, *half step*, narrow, and wide. They are increased and diminished according to the differences of these *passi*. One sometimes walks forward, and sometimes backwards, sometimes to the side, sometimes by traverse with one leg or with both. There are also those who withdraw the forward leg to void the body holding it suspended in air in order to respond with greater quickness.

OF THE PARRY

7. One parries as well with the right edge as, although seldomly, with the false edge, in a straight line as in an oblique line, sometimes with the point high or low, sometimes over or under. This will be according to whether he strikes by point or cut and whether with one weapon, the other weapon, or both together. Take heed that all the parries require an extended arm and will be accompanied with the right leg, followed by the left. When parrying with *dui tempi*: in the *tempo* that you parry, bring the left foot near to the right, and then in striking you will *pass* with the right forward.

OF THE *FEINTS* AND OF *COPRIR DELLA SPADA*

8. We call *feints* those deceptive signals of the sword that are made as well with the cut as with the point, outside and inside of the sword, above and below, forwards and backwards, and also in rotation as in a straight and oblique line, by the one and the other weapon. These *feints* strike directly to the opposite of where they signal. The *contrafinte* are done to counter the *feints*. The *coprir della spada* is a kind of *feint*. It is done by covering the point of the adversary's sword with the *debole* of your sword when you find him in low *quarta* and it must be done in a straight line.

OF CHANGING FROM *GUARD* TO *GUARD*

9. The changing from *guard* to *guard* can be done in three ways: directly, in reverse, and in exchange. The direct is when in *prima* I change to *seconda*, and from *seconda* to *terza*, or from *terza* to *quarta*. In reversing is when I go from *quarta* to *terza*, *terza* to *seconda* and from *seconda* to *prima*. In exchange is when I change from *prima* to *quarta* or from *quarta* to *prima*, and from *prima* to *terza* or from *terza* to *prima*, or else from *seconda* to *quarta* or from *quarta* to *seconda*. Therefore, be advised, when changing yourself from one *guard* to another while being at *measure*, one will go backwards with the left leg accompanied with the right to make you secure from the adversary.

AGAINST THOSE WHO CIRCLE

10. It could easily happen that the adversary *guadagnare* your sword from the inside while circling. Whereupon you will immediately *disengage* your sword from the outside carrying the left leg accompanied with the right to traverse toward the right part of your adversary, putting the point of your sword in a straight line so that it looks to the right shoulder of the enemy. As he comes from the outside to *guadagnare* once more, you will *disengage* under and strike him with a thrust in *quarta* advancing the right leg forward to *lunge*.

AGAINST THE *GUARD* OF LEFT FOOT

11. Finding the adversary in low *terza* and with the left foot forward, you will put yourself in *terza* also but with the right leg forward and sword's point crossed toward your left side. This is for two effects. One, he can not dominate your sword which he will seek with his dagger. The other is to uncover more of your body which will invite him to *pass*, and when he *passes* you will parry with the sword, *pass* with the point high in *terza* and stab him in the chest. Moreover, you want to be first to strike someone in the *guard* of the left foot. Place yourself to encounter him similarly in *terza* with the sword in a straight line, doing it so that the point looks to the enemy's dagger hand. At your convenience you will be able to give him a *stoccata* by *mezzo tempo* in the said hand. Alternatively, you will be able to make a *feint* over the dagger so he wants to parry, then you will *disengage* your sword below his dagger *passing* with the left foot forward. At the same time, find the enemy's sword with your dagger so you strike him by thrust below the arm. Moreover, you can feign to below the dagger so he similarly wants to parry, you will *disengage* and strike him from *seconda* above his dagger *passing* and parrying as above. Take heed that one can still feign and strike without *passing*, but only with the expectation that the adversary *feints* when you will have and then steps to strike. At this time, with only ceding the *vita* backwards in his *passing* and parrying your enemy's sword with your dagger, you will strike him from over or below his dagger, according to the occasion that you will see. If you have to face a left-hander who stands with his right foot forward, be warned that he must set himself into the encounter with his left foot, with the sword withdrawn low, and with the body inclined towards your right side. Carry your weapons to that same side, so that by doing this you will place the judgement of danger to the adversary. He will not be able to launch any attack that is not given in the defense.

ENGAGING THE SWORD

12. The sword is *engaged* for the purpose of coming to *measure* or to uncover the adversary. This is done from the outside and inside, high and low, but always in a *direct line* while the adversary firms or moves himself. Most of the time it is done in *dui tempi*. First, the *debole* of the sword is acquired with one *palmo* of the *debole* of yours. In the second *tempo* the beginning of the *forte* of the adversary's sword is acquired so that he will *disengage* and you will *counter-disengage* or not. Take heed that the sword faces in a *direct line* and that the *forte* always accompanies the *debole* together with the motion of the legs.

VERY USEFUL PRECEPT ABOUT DOMINATING THE SWORD

13. The sword is dominated in two ways. The first is when I have acquired the adversary's sword. I will not depart from the control at any time in striking. The second is when I have battered the sword in any way that makes it goes out of my presence, (in the *tempo* when it forcefully travels it is understood to be in my control) so I have the first strike while he rescues himself. The control of the single sword is from the stillness or motion, one is of the point and the other is the cut. It is dominated with the *forte* in parrying or it is beaten with the *debole* to seek the *tempo* and the *measure*. In single sword, having dominated the enemy's sword with the *forte*, you must never respond by cut, but by point it is good. Both can be done if you have dominated the enemy's sword with your sword and dagger together. In such *guard* rests the control, although I exhort you always to strike by point because it is more deadly and at no time is the sword removed from his presence. The cut does the opposite.

OF THE *DISENGAGE*, AND *COUNTER-DISENGAGE*

14. The *disengage* is moreover like the *counter-disengage*. It is done for escaping or for acquiring the *tempo* and the *measure*. It is done either forward or backwards, according to the said design. The method to *counter-disengage* requires following the sword of the adversary, replacing your sword to its first place. This can be done from one as from the other side. It is also necessary to know that the *disengage* of the sword can be performed from over or under the enemy's sword to *guadagnare* it. The difference between either *disengage* is thus: to *engage* by *disengage* from below is to *disengage* with a straight arm and with a little advancing of the foot. The *disengage* from above is done with the ceding of the *vita*, and with the arm and sword in an oblique line backwards. Then your sword will be free of the point of the enemy's sword, so replace your *forte* above his in an instant." This method of *disengaging* can be done to strike as much as to *engage*.

OF STRIKING

15. The strike is in two sorts, by cut or thrust. Each one of these has its diverse kinds according to its blow. The *mandritto* will be either *ordinario*, *fendente*, *tondo*, *montante*, *stramazzone*, *ridoppio* and from the riverse side they will be as above. The thrusts are converted into four kinds. The *mandritto* is that which commences from the right side, and these are called *ordinario* which are those that go through an oblique line, that is to say, from the left shoulder to the right knee of the enemy. However, those which go to strike by a straight line from up to down are called the *fendente*. The *tondo* requires that on the transverse it turns. Moreover the *montante* is that which departs with the right edge of the sword from below and proceeds to strike to the point of the adversary's left shoulder. *Stramazzone* is when the joint of the hand goes in the fashion of a wheel. It is called *ridoppio* when, with a *mezzo mandritto*, you cast down the enemy's sword then proceed to turn another *mandritto ordinario*. The *falso* can be determined in two manners: *dritto* and *manco*. The *falso dritto* can serve to knock the enemy's sword to the outside (i.e. towards his right side) and the *falso manco* knocks it towards his left side. Therefore, if you parry by *falso dritto*, I say it will be done much better by turning the joint of the hand and parrying with the right edge for more security, and so you will throw the *dritto* more quickly. However, when knocking it with the *falso manco* you can strike him by thrust as much as by cut. Take heed that when parrying with *falso*, parry with the middle of the sword up towards the point, and when parrying with the right edge, you shall parry with the *forte*, the middle of the sword down towards the hilt. Remember that the *mandritti* and *riversi* are done with a movement of the elbow and that when the *measure* and the *tempo* support it, with the upper part of the arm.

OF THE CUT

16. The cuts require to be done by scything. For in this manner all the *debole* comes to strike, so that little by little one will come to cut with the sharpest part of the edge. In these occasions the cuts that descend are stronger than those that are established from the waist upward. Concerning these said superior and inferior ways, they are found more or less at *measure*, being actions that offend by scything.

OF THE THRUST

17. The thrust are: the *stoccata*, the *imbroccata*, and the *punta riverso*. The *imbroccata* departs from the *prima guardia* and will go to strike the left shoulder of the adversary as far as to his right knee with the false edge underneath. One does not turn the hand because it will not arrive at the point of striking and must be hurled. The *stoccata* requires that it departs from the *terza guard* and it goes to strike the adversary towards the right shoulder. The *punta riversa* departs from the *quarta* and will go to strike from outside of the enemy's shoulder, well reversing the hand on the inside. Some come to the thrust in *falso* proceeding from low to high towards the chest of the adversary, retrieving the sword in low *guard*.

The Plates

METHOD OF PLACING THE HAND ON THE SWORD

The customs are not the same in all countries and many times enmities are practised with little integrity. In order to remain prepared for all these mishaps, it is not out of place to teach the method of placing the hand on the sword. First, we come to deal with its management. If by chance you have the right leg forward in placing your hand on the sword, bring that leg backwards and extend the right arm in high *prima* at the same time, as one of these figures shows. If you have the left leg forward, as the other figure shows, you can't draw forth the sword in the above said manner without changing the step. If you will make use of the sword and either cape, sword, or dagger, so also with single sword, the true method is by first placing the right step forward to present yourself in *quarta*. If the adversary is near, you will bring the left foot backwards presenting yourself as above. At this time, with your convenience, you will be able to grip the cape or dagger with more security, since the point of your sword will make it so that the adversary stands far away while you arrange your weapons. This is all I have to say on this.

I

DECLARATION OF THE *GUARDS*

As in any beautiful and wise writings, one can not make a composition without employing the letters of the alphabet. So too, in our art of fencing. Without the following *guards*, and some *scansi* and escaping of the *vita* (which come to be the foundation of this exercise), our use could not be demonstrated. Therefore the following six figures are marked alphabetically. A. shows you the *prima*, the *seconda* is presented by B., the *terza* by C., the *quarta* is named by D., the *quinta* by E., and the *sesta* by F.

2
D
A

3
B
F

4
C
E

A FIGURE DECLARED BY MEANS OF THE ALPHABET

A Figure that demonstrates being in *guard*, as it is shown in our art, and the incredible increasing of the *lunge*, with respect to the limbs that are all moved in striking.

- A The left shoulder in *guard*.
- B The knee of the left leg in *guard*.
- C The sole of the left foot in *guard*.
- D The *ordinary step* in *guard*.
- E The sole of the right foot in *guard*.
- F The thigh and the leg to the shoe in *guard*.
- G The hand of the right arm in *guard*.
- H The advancing of the right arm, with much more length.
- I The advancing of the right knee, almost a *passo*.
- K The advancing of the *passo*, little more of a foot.
- L The advancing of the left foot with its turn.
- M The advancing of the left knee by a *half step*.

5
H
A
G
B
I
M
F
E
K
D
L
C

METHOD OF *GUADAGNARE* THE SWORD INSIDE IN A STRAIGHT LINE AND STRIKING ACCORDING TO THE POINT WHICH THE ENEMY'S SWORD WILL PRESENT

There are two motives (it seems to me) for which it is necessary to *engage* the adversary. First, to *engage* the sword which is to seek the *measure* and *tempo*. The other, to engage the adversary's body which is to only seek the *measure*. These very good *engagements* are considered in the straight line. It is because there are two motives to *engage* that there shall also be two occasions. The first occasion, to *engage* with the sword, is in order to seek *measure* and *tempo* when the adversary is found in an oblique line. When you find the adversary with the sword in *quarta* such that it looks to your left side in an oblique line and your sword is to the outside, *disengage* with the increasing of the *passo* in order to *engage* on the inside in a straight line (as the figure shows). This should not be difficult because it is sufficient to only *engage* the sword in a straight line having found the adversary's sword in an oblique line. The second occasion, to *engage* the body, is only to seek *measure*. It is when the adversary is found in a straight line or with the body uncovered. Then, without *engaging* the sword to seek the *tempo*, it is sufficient to only *engage* the body with the straight line in order to find the *measure*, and then strike according to the point, although the use of the art requires that one *engages* the sword in all the lines without necessity. To strike according to the point one must always understand that when the adversary's sword point is in your presence, you will be able to strike directly in a straight line to where the height of the enemy's sword point will present. Whereupon, take one *palmo* from the point of the enemy's sword with the *forte* of your sword and you will strike securely. Be advised that if it is high, being even to your head, you will strike him in the face. If it should be even with your body you will be able to strike him in the face and in the chest. This is called striking according to the point which the enemy's sword will present. In these ways you will be able to *disengage* the sword securely from all sides to strike. When you *disengage*, carry the *forte* of your sword to the point of the adversary's sword in the first *tempo*, and it is not done as some masters do the *disengagement*. They do the *disengagement* in order to strike in the first *tempo*, coming with the point of their sword in the *forte* of the enemy's sword, not noticing that they give the point to the enemy and most of the time the offenses remain, as it is seen in our figures.

6
D
C

THE PRESENT AND SUBSEQUENT FIGURES DEMONSTRATE DIVERSE METHODS OF STRIKING FROM THE OUTSIDE

always presupposing the engagement on the inside, and the *disengagement* of your *Adversary's point to strike.*

In the subsequent figures, D. will have *engaged* the figure marked C. on the inside. C. will *disengage* to give D. a thrust in the chest. D will strike by thrust in the left eye, from *pie fermo* or by increasing of the *passo* as the figure demonstrates. Yet I also say that if C. should be a wise person, when he *disengaged* he would have *disengaged* to *feint* with the *vita* held back somewhat. D. will surely proceed to strike C. C. will parry by *falso* or true edge from outside the enemy's sword to give a *dritto* to the face or an *imbroccata* in the chest and afterwards C. should retire in low *quarta*.

7
C
D

FIGURES THAT SHOW HOW MUCH OF THE *MEASURE* IS LOST TO ATTACK THE LEGS

The figure D. will have *guadagnare* figure C's sword. C. turns a *riverso* to D's leg. In the turning of the *riverso*, D. can strike by *stramazzone* to the arm or a thrust to the face if he throws it excessively forward while retiring the right leg backwards in striking as the figure shows. However, I say that when D. *engages* C's sword, C. should have been a wise person and discharged a *riverso* to the face accompanied with a *dritto fendente* to the head and this would have been more secure.

8
C
D

FIGURE THAT STRIKES WITH *PASSATA* WHILE THE ADVERSARY *DISENGAGES* TO STRIKE

The figure D. will have *guadagnare* figure C's sword on the inside. At the same time, figure C. *disengages* to give figure D. a *stoccata* in the face. D. strikes in the face from *seconda* with a *passata*, hitting while catching the hilt of the enemy's sword with the left hand. However, I am not defective to say that if C. were a wise person, he should have *disengaged* the sword to *feint* with the *vita* held somewhat backwards. As D. surely comes to *pass*, C. can *afalsar* underneath the enemy's sword and quarter his body with the *scanso della vita*, by passing the leg crossed backwards to strike him in the chest.

9
C
D

FIGURE THAT STRIKES FROM *QUARTA* IN THE PAP UNDER THE RIGHT ARM WHILE THE ADVERSARY *DISENGAGES* TO STRIKE

The figure D. will have *guadagnare* figure C's sword. Figure C. will turn a *riverso* to D's face. D. strikes in the rotating of the *riverso* by *quarta* in the chest under the sword arm, raising up the arm and sword hilt while well increasing the *passo*, as you see. Therefore, I say that in changing to turn the *riverso* C. would have *disengaged* the sword backwards with retiring somewhat while raising the sword in an oblique line so that the point looks towards the adversary's left side, then D. would want to enter from *quarta*. C. will parry with a *mezzo mandritto* to give a *riverso* to the face or a thrust in the chest.

10

METHOD OF STRIKING UNDER THE ENEMY'S SWORD IN DIVERSE ACTIONS

First, from *terza*, you will put yourself in high *quarta* traversed so that your sword's point is equal to the adversary's left shoulder. He will come to cover yours in an oblique line. As he comes you will turn the hand into *seconda* folding and lowering the body so that you strike by *contratempo* in the body from under his sword as the figure shows. Second, in the case that the adversary has you *engaged* on the outside, you *disengage* to *feint* a thrust to the face in *quarta* so he will want to parry. You will turn the hand with the same folding to strike him under the sword as in above. Third, if you were *engaged* on the inside, you can *disengage* to *feint* a thrust to the face in *terza*. He will raise his sword to parry and you will strike him under the sword, by turning your hand into *seconda* in the same manner above. Fourth, if you *engage* your adversary from the inside and he *disengages* to strike you with a thrust in the face, you will be able to strike him in two manners. First, you can strike him by *contratempo* in his coming, lowering the *vita* and the sword in *terza*. Yet you can also strike him by parrying in *terza* with the point high then turning the hand into *seconda* to strike in the same manner above. Fifth and finally, if you should *engage* your adversary from the outside and he *disengages* to *engage* your sword on the inside, in the same *tempo* turn the hand with lowering and folding the *vita*. You will strike him by *terza* under the sword in the same method which is above.

II
D
C

FIGURE THAT PARRIES WITH THE SWORD AND BOTH HANDS TO STRIKE BY *PASSATA* WITH A THRUST IN THE THROAT WHILE THE ADVERSARY *DISENGAGES* THE SWORD

The figure D. will have *guadagnare* figure C's sword on the inside in low *guard*. Figure C. will *disengages* to give D. a *stoccata* in the chest. D. will *pass* with the left leg in the same *tempo* pressing down the enemy's sword with both hands to strike him in the chest in *terza*. However, there is no doubt that if C. had been an intelligent person when he *disengaged* the point to strike, he should have *disengaged* somewhat held back. D. will parry and *pass* with with both the hands to strike C. C. only needs to lower the sword's point towards the earth and turn the hand into *seconda* along with voiding the *vita* somewhat toward the adversary's left side to *disengage* the edge over the enemy's sword. C. will strike him from the inside with a *riverso* to the face and withdraw in *terza*. Another option is to parry and *pass* with the left leg to the inside right, turn the *vita* and take his sword with both hands. In the turn give D. a thrust in the chest so he will not be able to redress.

12
D
C

FIGURE THAT STRIKES WITH A *SCANNATURA* BY THRUSTING IN THE RIGHT FLANK AND *PASSATA* WHILE THE ADVERSARY *DISENGAGES* TO STRIKE

This method of striking, called the *scannatura*, is done in the following manner. Figure C. has *engaged* D's sword on the outside. Figure D. *disengages* a thrust to C's face. Figure C. encounters the enemy's sword from the outside while lowering the point into *seconda* and *passing* the left leg in the same *tempo* to strike in the flank. C. lowers the hilt and body to catch the hand as seen in the illustration.

C
D

FIGURE THAT STRIKES UNDER THE ENEMY'S SWORD BY *CONTRATEMPO* WITHOUT PARRYING

with only lowering the body as the figure shows

The figure D. will have *guadagnare* figure C's sword on the inside. Figure C. *disengages* to give D. a *stoccata* in the face. D. lowers the body and advances the right leg in the same *tempo* to strike him by *contratempo* without parrying from *seconda* under the enemy's sword as the figure shows. Alternatively, you can succeed when C. *disengages* to give D. a *stoccata* in the face. D. parries by *terza* with the point high, and in the same *tempo* lowers the point and turns the sword into *seconda*. He would be able to strike by *passata* in the chest together with catching the sword hand. However, if C. were a practical person, in their coming C. would only retire the right foot backwards and meet the enemy's sword on the outside. In the same *tempo* he lowers the point and turns the hand into *seconda* to strike by *scannatura* under the enemy's sword. Otherwise, in his retiring he will parry with the left hand from up to down under his arm and strike D. from high *seconda* in the chest or face.

14
C
D

TWOFOLD METHODS TO *GUADGNARE* THE ADVERSARY'S SWORD ON THE INSIDE AND OUTSIDE

Understanding from experience how useful it is to know the *guadagnare* of the enemy's sword, I do not want to neglect explaining the method one shall keep the same to *engage* and *guadagnare*. First, proceeding to *engage* the adversary's sword on either the inside or outside, one shall first *engage* from the same distance (about one *palmo* from the point). Remember, to *engage* on the inside make the sword's point look to the adversary's right shoulder, and on the outside it looks to his left shoulder. That being done, proceed towards the adversary's sword so he will *disengage*. In that instant *counter-disengage* turning the sword to its place, or with the same *counter-disengage* one will strike in the *tempo* of his *disengage*. Moreover, if the adversary comes to *engage* the sword, on the inside as on the outside, such that it is found in a level straight line with the arm extended, in that instant *disengage* and *engage* traveling forward. If it happens that one has to *disengage* to *engage* on the inside, carry the right foot forward in the *disengage*, folding the body toward your right side bringing the left hand next to the right then *pass* with the left foot to strike in *quarta* with a thrust in the chest. *Disengaging* to *engage* on the outside is similarly done by bringing the right foot forward while bending the body towards your left side and *passing* with the left foot to strike in *seconda* in the chest.

Next, be advised the following figures demonstrate *engaging* on the outside of the sword in *terza*. You shall hold to the method of *guadagnare* the adversary's sword as said above.

15
D
C

THE PRESENT AND SUBSEQUENT FIGURES SHOW DIVERSE METHODS TO STRIKE ON THE INSIDE ALWAYS

presupposing the engagement on the outside and the disengagement of your Adversary's point to strike

The subsequent figures show diverse methods to strike on the inside, always presupposing your engagement on the outside so the adversary *disengages* to strike you. D. *disengages* as above so C. will strike him in *quarta* from *pie fermo*, or in the throat and face by increasing of the *passo*. Yet if D. were an intelligent person he should have *disengaged* beating the enemy's sword with the edge to give C. a thrust to the face or *riverso* to the arm then withdraw himself in *terza* by *ordinary step*.

16
D
C

FIGURE THAT STRIKES NEXT TO THE EAR WITH THE *SCANSO DEL PIE DRITTO*

The figure C. will *engage* B. on the outside. B. *disengages* to strike C. in *quarta*. C. strikes in the face next to the ear with the *scanso del pie dritto* traversed on the outside of his sword. Nonetheless there is no defect to say that if B. were a practical person he should have *disengaged* the sword to *feint* with the *vita* withdrawn somewhat backwards. C. will surely come to strike with his *scanso del pie dritto* traversed to B. B. would encounter the enemy's sword from the outside lowering the point into *seconda* and *passing* with the left leg in a same *tempo* to strike him in the flank, hitting by catching the sword hand.

17
B
C

FIGURE THAT STRIKES FROM *QUARTA* IN THE THROAT BY *PASSATA* OF THE LEFT FOOT

The figure C. will have *engaged* figure B's sword on the outside. Figure B. will *disengage* to give C. a *stoccata* in the face. In the *disengage* C. strikes from *quarta* by *passata* in the throat or face as the figure shows. Yet if B. were a practical person he would have *disengaged* the sword to *feint* with the *vita* withdrawn somewhat backwards and as C. surely comes to *pass* with the *quarta*, B. would quarter with the *scanso della vita*, passing with the left leg behind to the right to strike in the chest.

18
B
C

FIGURE THAT STRIKES FROM *QUARTA* WITH THE *SCANSO DELLA VITA* CARRYING THE LEFT LEG CROSSED BEHIND TO THE RIGHT

The figure C. has *guadagnare* D's sword on the outside. D. *disengages* to give C. a thrust in the face. C. strikes from *quarta* with the *scanso della vita*, passing with the left leg behind and crossing to the right, as the figure shows. Yet if D. should be a practical person he should have *disengaged* to *guadagnare* C's sword on the inside together with folding the body towards his right side. Having *guadagnare*, in an instant he should *pass* the left foot forward giving a thrust from *quarta* in the chest. Alternatively, he could have *disengaged* with a *mezzo mandritto* to batter the enemy's sword, giving C. a *riverso* to the face, withdrawing in *terza* and thus be made secure.

19
D
C

FIGURE THAT STRIKES IN THE FACE FROM *SECONDA* BY *PASSATA*, HITTING WHILE CATCHING THE ENEMY'S SWORD ARM WITH THE LEFT HAND

In the following figures C. has *engaged* the figure D. on the outside. D. *disengages* to give C. a *stoccata*. C. parries the enemy's sword by *quarta* while beating the right foot along with *passing* and turning the body to strike in the face from *seconda* all in one *tempo*. This can also be done without *passing* and striking him from *quarta*, albeit by *dui tempi*. Yet if D. were a practical person in the interplay of the sword, when C. *disengaged* to parry D. by *quarta* with the beating of the right foot, D. should have *counter-disengaged* his sword to the outside and strike him from *seconda* in the face, then withdraw backwards in *terza*. Follow the enemy's sword with your sword in such withdrawing. Thus D. should rest having struck C.

20
D
C

SWORD AND DAGGER FIGURE WHICH DEMONSTRATES THE METHOD OF *ENGAGING* THE ADVERSARY'S SWORD WHEN YOUR IN HIGH *PRIMA* ON THE INSIDE

Take heed that if the point of the enemy's sword looks towards your right shoulder you shall take it outside and the same method will be kept to guadagnare the low guards

The following figures show the interplay of sword and dagger, and principally teaches the method of *engaging* the adversary's sword. It is not possible in one figure to show all the methods of *engaging* on the outside and inside, low and high when you're in high *prima*, so refer to what is described to the reader. Take heed that if the point of the enemy's sword looks towards your right side you will take it on the outside. Moreover, you *engage* the low *guards* with the sword in a perpendicular line, either *terza* or *quarta*.

21
D
A

FIGURES SHOWING THAT WITH ONLY ONE PARRY OF THE DAGGER IT IS POSSIBLE TO STRIKE IN THREE PLACES BY THRUST: THE FACE, CHEST, AND THIGH

These following figures show you an artful manner of striking in three diverse methods by thrust with only one parry of the dagger which is done like this. Having *engaged* the adversary from *quarta* on the inside (in whatever *guard* is apt to *engage* on the inside) he will be able to *disengage* to hit you in two ways: in the face and chest. Having *disengaged* to strike you, you will parry his sword on the inside with your dagger above your right arm. In the first case you can strike high or low in the face, chest (under the arm), or thigh. In the second case you can only strike in the face and thigh.

22
C
D

FIGURE THAT STRIKES FROM *SECONDA* IN THE CHEST WITH A *FEINT* BETWEEN THE WEAPONS *DISENGAGING* OVER THE DAGGER. IN THE SAME MANNER YOU SHOULD BE ABLE TO STRIKE FROM *QUARTA*

Finding the adversary in low *terza* with the arm withdrawn and dagger forward united with the sword, place yourself to encounter in high *terza*, making the *feint* in high *quarta* or in the same *terza*, on the outside of his dagger towards the face. While he raises the dagger to parry and strike you from *quarta*, you will *disengage* over his dagger and in the same *tempo* of parrying on the inside, you will strike him from *seconda* in the chest.

23
E
C

FIGURE THAT STRIKES ABOVE THE RIGHT ARM IN THE CHEST AND MAKES THE SWORD FALL BY PRYING IT LOOSE WITH SWORD AND DAGGER.

From these figures you can easily comprehend and learn the method of casting the sword from the hand, while also giving a thrust to the chest in the same *tempo*. You begin in *terza* with the arm withdrawn and the dagger united with the sword. The adversary can be in the same *guard* or in *quarta*. You will *engage* his sword on the inside in *quarta* and allow your dagger to lower to the middle of the right arm in an oblique line. When the adversary *disengages* to strike you in the chest from *quarta*, you will strike his body with a *punta riversa* from the outside, somewhat raising the hilt of your sword and in the same *tempo* parrying with the flat of your dagger from the outside to below it. This will cause him to abandon the weapon by force.

24

FIGURE THAT PARRIES WITH THE DAGGER HIGH ON THE INSIDE AND STRIKES BY *RIVERSO* IN THE THIGH AND FROM *QUARTA* IN THE CHEST AS THE FIGURES SHOW

Finding yourself in *quarta* with the dagger high and your adversary is in any *guard* apt to *engage* on the inside (also with the right leg forward). Begin to *engage* on the inside in *quarta* and he will *disengage* to strike you from *quarta* in the face. You will parry from the inside with your dagger above your right arm, so you are able to strike him in the thigh with a *riverso*, or under the arm in *quarta*.

25
C
D

FIGURE THAT PARRIES WITH THE SWORD FROM *QUARTA* ACCOMPANIED WITH THE DAGGER AND STRIKES HIM FROM *QUARTA* IN THE FACE OR BY A *RIVERSO* IN THE ARM AS THE FIGURE SHOWS

If you are in extended *terza* with the dagger at your wrist and the adversary is in any *guard* apt to *engage* on the outside, you will begin to *engage* him in either high or low *terza* without moving the dagger from its place. The adversary will *disengage* to strike you from *quarta* or *seconda*. You will be able to strike by *riverso* in the arm or *quarta* in the face after parrying in *quarta* with the sword and dagger.

26
D
C
RA. F

FIGURE THAT *FEINTS* ABOVE THE DAGGER AND AS THE ADVERSARY RAISES TO PARRY IT, STRIKES HIM IN THE CHEST BY *DISENGAGING* UNDER THE SWORD FROM *QUARTA*

Finding yourself in extended *terza* with the dagger at the wrist and the adversary is in low *quarta* with the sword withdrawn and the dagger extended high, begin to make a *feint* in *terza* above his dagger. Keep your dagger in its place while he parries you upward with the dagger. You will strike in that same *tempo* from *quarta* or *seconda*. *Disengage* under the dagger and parry together with your attack to strike him in the chest with *quarta*.

27
E
C

FIGURE THAT PARRIES WITH THE DAGGER UNDER HIS RIGHT ARM AND STRIKES FROM *SECONDA* IN THE FACE, OR WITH A *STRAMAZZONE RIVERSO* IN THE SWORD ARM

Finding yourself in low or high *terza* with the dagger at the wrist and the adversary in any *guard* convenient to *engage* from the outside, you will begin to *engage* from the outside with high or low *terza*, raising the dagger according to the occasion. He will want to *disengage* to the inside and thrust from *quarta* or *seconda*. You will parry down with the dagger under your sword arm and throw a *stramazzone* to the arm or strike from *seconda* in the face as shown.

28
D
C

FIGURE THAT STRIKES FROM *SECONDA* ABOVE THE DAGGER IN THE LEFT SHOULDER WHILE THE ADVERSARY SEEKS TO *GUADAGNARE* THE SWORD FROM THE OUTSIDE

Find yourself in extended *terza* with the dagger in an oblique line above the beginning of your sword's *forte*. The adversary is in the same *terza guard* and comes to *engage* from the outside. You will *disengage* and beat his sword from *quarta* with your sword and, all in one *tempo*, parry the already oppressed sword immediately with the dagger so you strike above his dagger in the left shoulder in the same *tempo*.

29
C
C

FIGURE THAT STRIKES FROM *SECONDA* ABOVE THE DAGGER IN THE LEFT SHOULDER WITH A *FEINT*, WHILE PARRYING FROM UP TO DOWN WITH THE DAGGER UNDER HIS RIGHT ARM

You are in *terza* or *quarta* with the arm withdrawn and the dagger at your wrist. The adversary is in *quarta* with the sword withdrawn and the dagger extended high. Now make a *feint* under his dagger and raise yours. He will parry with the dagger down towards his left side. You will *disengage* above his dagger in the same *tempo* as parrying the enemy's sword from the inside under your right arm, so you will strike from *seconda* above his dagger.

30
C
F

FIGURE THAT STRIKES WITH A *PASSATA* IN THE CHEST BY AN ASCENDING *FALSO* THRUST IN BETWEEN THE WEAPONS WHILE PARRYING WITH THE DAGGER ABOVE HIS RIGHT ARM AND BINDING THE WEAPONS TOGETHER WELL

Finding the adversary in *terza* with both weapons extended in an oblique line (so the enemy's sword point looks to your right shoulder and the dagger to your left), place yourself to encounter in *terza* with the sword's point low and dagger high while bending the body as much as possible towards your left side. He will approach to *engage* you for some design of his. You will *pass* with the left foot towards his right side in the same *tempo* and parry with the dagger inside above your right arm to drive forth an ascending *falso* thrust in between his weapons. Alternatively, *disengage* with both weapons keeping the sword above and press the sword to strike him from *terza* in the same *tempo*.

31
F
C

FIGURE THAT USES THE *AFALSAR* TO STRIKE IN THE MOUTH BY *QUARTA* WHILE LOWERING THE DAGGER TO PARRY. THE ADVERSARY *DISENGAGES* HIS SWORD SEEKING TO PARRY WITH THE DAGGER

Finding the adversary in high *terza* with the dagger crossed and united at the commencement of the *forte* of his sword somewhat obliquely, you will *engage* him with *terza* from the outside keeping the dagger high. He will *disengage* under while parrying with the dagger in order to strike you from *quarta*. You will parry with the dagger down towards your left and in one *tempo disengage* under his dagger so you will strike him from *quarta* in the face or wherever it happens most easily.

32
C
C

FIGURE THAT STRIKES IN THE CHEST FROM *QUARTA* UNDER THE DAGGER, CARRYING THE RIGHT LEG BACK AND PARRYING HIGH WITH THE DAGGER. THE ADVERSARY WILL BE *PASSING* FORWARD TO STRIKE FROM *SECONDA* ABOVE THE DAGGER

The adversary is in low *terza*, so place yourself to encounter in high *terza* keeping the dagger united and crossed above your *forte*. He comes with a *passata* in order to strike you from *seconda* above your dagger and parries wide with his. You withdraw the right leg backwards and, as he raises his dagger to parry, will *disengage* under his dagger, carrying the body well forward as the figure shows to strike him from *quarta*.

33
C
E

FIGURE THAT STRIKES FROM *SECONDA* ABOVE THE DAGGER IN THE CHEST WHILE THE ADVERSARY *PASSES* WITH THE LEFT FOOT. THE STRIKE IS SOLELY BY WITHDRAWING THE RIGHT LEG BACKWARDS IN HIS COMING AND PARRYING WITH THE DAGGER UNDER THE RIGHT ARM

The adversary is in *quarta* with the sword withdrawn and low but the dagger extended high and wide. Place yourself to encounter in *quarta* with the arm extended and dagger high. He moves with a *passata* to parry your sword down to strike from *seconda*. You will withdraw your right leg backwards and parry with the dagger down towards your right side while *disengaging* your sword above his dagger to strike from *seconda*.

34
D
F

FIGURE THAT STRIKES IN THE CHEST WITH A THRUST BETWEEN THE WEAPONS *DISENGAGING* ABOVE THE DAGGER, WHILE THE ADVERSARY'S DAGGER IS IN *GUARDIA LARGA*, FORSAKING THE ENEMY'S ARRIVAL AT *MEASURE*

Finding the adversary in *quarta* with the arm withdrawn and the dagger high, straight, and wide with an extended arm, you will proceed to encounter him in extended *terza* with the dagger crossed in front of your chest. You will approach from outside of his dagger, arriving so that you make the point of your sword even with his dagger. As he firms himself in *guard* you will *disengage* from *quarta* above *lunging* to strike him in the chest.

35
F
C

METHOD OF USING THE SWORD AND CAPE

To better understand the cape, here are some points about using it. Having the cape about you, it will descend down from the right shoulder until at the middle of the left arm. Turning the left hand to the outside, wrap the cape over the arm, placing yourself in *terza* with it, or another guard as it pleases you. The *footwork* will be done in this method: proceeding with the sword and dagger is the same except in the parry, considering that the cape can be cut and pierced which can not be done to the dagger. Encountering your adversary in *terza*, as above: when he throws a *mandritto* to your head you will *pass* forward with the left foot in the same *tempo*, parrying with the cape in the *forte* of the enemy's sword and driving a thrust into the chest. One can also parry the said blow from *prima*, with the sword in *guardia di testa* accompanied with the cape. In this *tempo* gather the left foot near to the right and immediately proceed with the right forward to turn a *mandritto* to the head or leg. Yet, when a *mandritto* or *riverso* is thrown at the leg, one can just pull the right foot backwards to give a *riverso* in the sword arm (if attacked by *mandritto*) or a *dritto* in the sword arm (if he does a *riverso*). However, the true parry is done by parrying with the sword. You will strike securely when the sword proceeds with the cape pushing the enemy's sword. The following figures demonstrate the method that must be kept to *guadagnare* the adversary's sword from the inside in sword and cape.

36
D
D

FIGURE THAT STRIKES WITH *COUNTER-DISENGAGING* FROM *QUARTA* IN THE FACE PARRYING THE ENEMY'S SWORD ON THE OUTSIDE WITH THE CAPE ARM WHILE THE ADVERSARY *DISENGAGES* HIS SWORD IN ORDER TO STRIKE WITH A THRUST

Your adversary is in *quarta* with the sword extended and high, and high. Present yourself to *engage* it from *quarta* on the inside with the cape arm under your *forte*. He will *disengage* to strike you with a thrust in any way. Parry it up with the cape to outside of your left side and *counter-disengage* from *quarta*, so you will strike in the face or wherever it is easiest."

37
D
D

FIGURE THAT STRIKES THE LEFT-HANDER WITH *STRAMAZZONE RIVERSO* IN THE FACE AND CAN ALSO STRIKE HIM FROM *SECONDA* IN THE CHEST, OR WITH A *QUARTA* FROM OUTSIDE OF THE ENEMY'S SWORD IN THE *DISENGAGE* OF HIS POINT TO STRIKE

Finding the left handed adversary in *quarta* with the arm extended, you will begin to *engage* on the inside of his sword with *terza* and the dagger high. He *disengages* to strike you from *seconda* in the face. You will be able to strike in three manners. First, by lowering only the dagger to parry his sword you will strike him with a *stramazzone riverso* in the face or from *seconda* in the chest. Be advised that in his *disengagement* it would be better to strike him from *quarta* with only the sword from the outside.

38
D
C

FIGURE THAT PARRIES HIS HEAD WITH THE SWORD'S POINT HIGH AND DAGGER CROSSED INSIDE HIS SWORD AT THE *FORTE* SO THAT HE WILL BE ABLE TO STRIKE IN TWO MANNERS, FIRST WITH A THRUST IN THE FACE OR WITH A *RIVERSO* IN THE LEG

I would have certainly done injustice to myself if I had not revealed this noble parry (or true defense) which defends the noble parts of the body. Therefore, I ascribe the present figures. One is found in *prima* and the other in *quinta*. From *quinta*, with only raising the arm while turning the hand into *quarta* and increasing the *passo* he can proceed to *guadagnare* the adversary's sword on the inside. The enemy can *disengage* by rotating under the sword to throw a *dritto fendente* to the same figure. That same figure will be able to strike the adversary securely in two places (a thrust in the face or cut in the leg) by only turning into *seconda* with the point high and putting the dagger inside the sword's *forte*. This is shown well by the two lines descending from the sword's point, one goes down into the head and the other into the thigh.

39
E
A

FIGURE THAT STRIKES WITH A THRUST FROM *TERZA* IN THE THIGH AND WITH THE DAGGER IN THE BODY WHILE THE ADVERSARY *DISENGAGES* TO STRIKE WITH A *RIVERSO* TO THE LEG

Seeing this figure struck with the sword and also the dagger, this may appear difficult to some. This explanation will easily prove the method. Finding both adversaries in *quarta* with the right edge of their swords touching and the points similarly aimed at the face of the adversary, one is forced to press the sword, same as the enemy. Feeling the adversary press, one will resolve to turn a *riverso* to the leg. The same adversary can suddenly lower the sword and turn the hand into *terza* with a *pass* of the left leg forward to strike him with the sword and dagger while parrying with the sword as the figure shows.

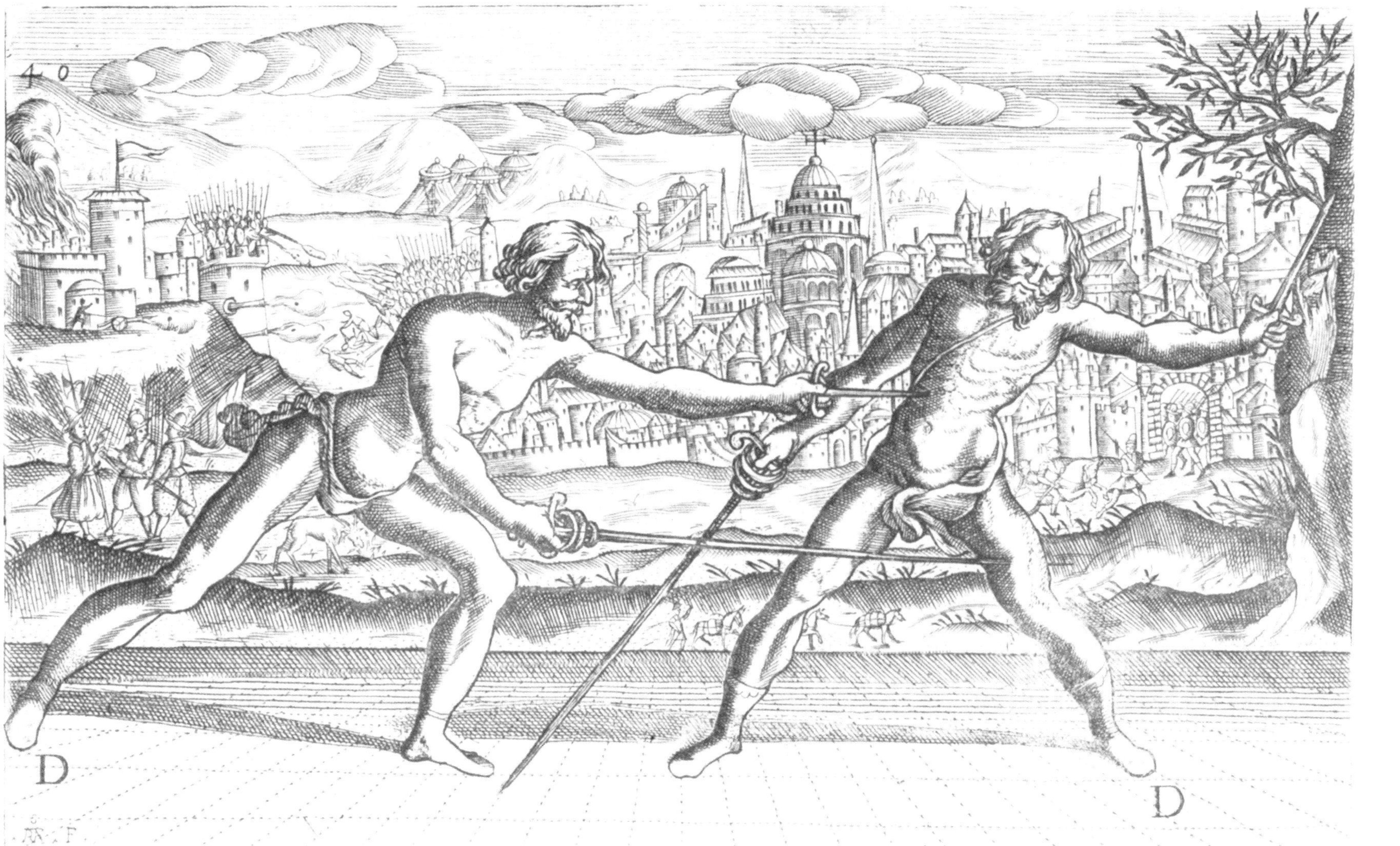
40
D
D

FIGURE THAT PARRIES THE *STRAMAZZONE RIVERSO* WITH THE SWORD TO IMMEDIATELY PASS FORWARD WITH THE LEFT FOOT AND STAB UNDER THE RIGHT ARM IN THE PAP

It is well noted that when the adversary thrust you should parry it with dagger (on the inside as on the outside) to *stramazzone riverso* in the enemy's sword arm. When you thrust at your adversary, he should parry you from the inside towards your left side and will turn the said *stramazzone* at you. Parry with the sword in *terza* from the outside, immediately *passing* the left leg forward to place your dagger above the enemy's sword so you will strike him from *seconda* with a thrust in the chest. To declare the following figures, I say that the adversary is in *terza* with the dagger at the *forte* of his sword and the other is in the *settima guard* with the dagger arm extended forward and the sword somewhat low and withdrawn to him. This latter figure being at *measure* will have thrown a thrust above the dagger, and the enemy will parry to the outside towards his left side then respond with a *stramazzone riverso*. However, the same latter figure in that instant will parry with *quarta* and *pass* with the left foot forward to strike him with the dagger as the figure shows. Wanting to return backwards, he will retire the left leg while turning a *riverso* in the adversary's sword arm in the same *tempo* to return into the same *guard*.

4
C

METHOD OF KNOWING HOW TO PROFIT WELL FROM THE *ROTELLA* FINDING YOURSELF AGAINST ANOTHER *ROTELLA*

It very often happens that one's own weapons make war to those who do not know their use well. Therefore, it is not outside of my purpose to mention some particulars of the *rotella*. It is a most perilous weapon to those who have not done any kind of practice. The *rotella* must be held embraced with the left arm somewhat curved, in a way that looks somewhat towards your left side, but not so curved that it impedes the eye so that you cannot discern whatever part of the enemy you want to proceed to strike. Therefore, finding the enemy with the sword extended forward in *guardia stretta*, one shall first *engage* the enemy's sword, from the inside or from the outside according to the occasion, and then increase with the left step pushing the already *guadagnare* sword with the *rotella* and strike from *terza* with an ascending thrust from the wrist. Alternatively, if the enemy is found in *guardia larga* and throws a *dritto* or *riverso* to the leg, you must parry with a *falso* (the *dritto* as the *riverso*) and respond with a cut to the adversary's legs. However, if he should throw a thrust or cut to the dome of the face or head, you will be able to parry with the *rotella* when the cut or thrust comes without a *feint*. The *rotella* is heavy so to be assured from the *feint* one can not parry with the quickness that can be done with the *targa* or *brocchieri*. Therefore, do not parry in such a method with the *rotella*. Consider this, if the same figure wants to parry the adversary's thrust to outside of his *rotella*, he will necessarily block his sight in that parry. Being thus impeded, in that instant the enemy will have the opportunity to *pass* with the left foot forward and with strike (as the figure shows) in the chest or base of the body without the sword's motion being seen. However, the same figure could parry with the sword from *seconda* or *quarta* (according to the occasion), then increase the left step to push the enemy's sword with the *rotella* and strike from *terza* with an ascending thrust to be more secure.

42
F
E

FIGURE THAT STRIKES UNDER THE *ROTELLA* WHILE THE ADVERSARY SEEKS TO PARRY WITH HIS *ROTELLA* TO STRIKE WITH A THRUST IN THE CHEST

When one is found at blows with his enemy, much attention is needed to the deceptions and *feints* found in the weapons. The following figures will demonstrate how most of the times the parry is dangerous when one parries and does not respond in the same *tempo*. It is also seen demonstrated in this action of the *rotella*. One is in *quinta* with the arm perpendicular and sword's point low with the *rotella* forward by the chest. The enemy is in *sesta* with the *rotella* arm extended forward and sword somewhat back. The same one will approach at *measure* to thrust outside of the *rotella* to the face. As he raises the *rotella* to parry, his view will be obscured. The same one will *afalsar* the sword under the *rotella* to strike him from *quarta* as the figure shows. Yet if he should be a practical person when the adversary thrust for the face he should parry, extending the arm of the *rotella* and *passing* with the left foot forward, immediately folding the body and head towards his right side to give him a thrust to the chest. Alternatively, when the adversary has thrown the thrust, he should have parried with the sword in *quarta* and in an instant *passed* with the left foot forward and push the enemy's sword with the *rotella*. He would have struck him from *terza* with an ascending thrust in the body and thus it would be done securely.

43
F
E

Some Terms of the Cut

I had resolved to present some figures which show many results of the method of striking and parrying by cut. I then considered that which I can do with figures can also be done with the following few advisements. Finding the adversary in *terza* or *quarta* so that the sword's point looks to the middle of your body. You will place yourself to encounter him in *quarta* with the sword's point somewhat high and traversed towards your right side. You will approach towards the adversary's sword somewhat to throw a *dritto* at his sword accompanied with a descending *riverso* to the face. On the contrary, when the enemy turns a *riverso* to the face you will *pass*, parrying with your dagger in *guardia di faccia* above your right arm to give him a thrust from *terza* in the chest. Alternatively, having parried and *passed* as above, you can give him a *dritto* to the leg. Moreover, you will be able to parry the said *riverso* with the sword from *quarta* and *pass*, with as shown in the figure that strikes with the dagger under the adversary's arm*, parrying with the dagger to strike him with a *riverso* to the legs or in the pap with the dagger in the same method. Moreover, you will also be able to place yourself in *quarta* with the sword's point low showing the *vita* somewhat, and as he comes from the outside to thrust at you, parry upwards with a *falso* of the sword upwards to give him a *dritto* to the face or a thrust in the chest. Yet if the adversary comes to batter your sword (from the inside or outside), you will do thus: if he throws a *dritto* at the sword, in the same *tempo* turn a *riverso* to the face. If he throws a *riverso* to the outside by battering the sword, in the same *tempo* turn a *dritto* to the face. Take heed that when parrying the *dritto* or *riverso* to the head, parry in the same method shown in the figure which parries with the sword crossed with the dagger on the inside at the *forte* (it has two lines, one descending to the face and the other to the thigh).* If the adversary throws either a *dritto* or *riverso* at your lower parts, you will parry from *seconda* with the sword's point low. If he does a *dritto*, you will parry and *disengage* with the edge over the enemy's sword, placing your dagger above the said sword to give him a *riverso* to the arm. If he does a *riverso*, you will parry on the outside in the same method giving him a thrust in the chest, then place the dagger in the same *tempo* above the adversary's sword. This is as much as it occurs to me to say concerning this.

* Refering to the action illustrated in plate 41.

* Refering to the action illustrated in plate 39.

SECURE METHOD OF DEFENDING YOURSELF FROM ALL KINDS OF BLOWS WITH A PARRY OF *RIVERSO* AND ALWAYS STRIKING BY *IMBROCCATA*

Desiring to end my work with this, it does not seem out of the purpose to close with this brief discourse only consisting of demonstrating the virtue and action of the *prima* and *quarta guardia*. Finding in the *prima* the offense and in the *quarta* the defense; beginning and ending whatsoever honorable quarrel considering that the *quarta* defends from whatever resolute or irresolute blow and the *prima* offends the adversary. Therefore it is necessary to say (by both being most faithful companions) that the beginning of the one is the end of the other. Without beginning there is no end because the beginning proceeds to the ending. In as much, the *prima* will commence from high and finish in *quarta* somewhat low. This is for two reasons. First, because if the adversary throws a thrust or a cut *passing* with the left foot somewhat, parry with a *riverso* towards the adversary's right side and drive forth the right foot so you can strike by *imbroccata* in the chest. With such an ending return into the *quarta guardia*. Second, because the adversary can only offend to the right side, so this defense comes easily by ascending the said *quarta*. Therefore, with demonstrating courage in such actions, the eye quickly recognizes the uncovered and covered parts of the adversary, strength and quickness in the legs, arms, and hands, quickness in the parry and striking, and agility in the *vita*. This is the nature of the *prima* and *quarta guardia*.

I, Brother Gregory *Lombardellis*, Doctor of Theology of Sienna and Consultor of the Holy Office of the Inquisition in the City of the Siennese, have seen this work firsthand, in which I have found nothing which may be contrary to the faith or to good customs. Therefore, it seems to me that it may be ordered to press.

Imprimatur by Brother Archang. Inquisitor of the Siennese
Fabius Picolomineis Vic.
Cosmus Talias Audit

AT SIENNA IN THE YEAR FROM THE BIRTH OF CHRIST 1610

SOLD in the house of the noble and most diligent man, *Camillus Turus*